the great
GENERATIONAL
TRANSITION

practical
insight for
every leader

DARLENE ZSCHECH

www.DARLENEZSCHECH.com

the great generational transition

Published by EWI Inc, PO Box 6049, Baulkham Hills NSW 2153, Australia.

Unless otherwise identified, Scripture quotations are from the HOLY BIBLE, NEW INTERNATIONAL VERSION®. Copyright © 1973, 1978, 1984 International Bible Society. Used by permission of Zondervan Publishing House. All rights reserved.

Scripture quotations marked (AMP) are taken from the Amplified Bible, Copyright © 1954, 1958, 1962, 1964, 1965, 1987 by The Lockman Foundation. Used by permission.

Scripture quotations from THE MESSAGE. Copyright © by Eugene H. Peterson 1993, 1994, 1995, 1996, 2000, 2001, 2002. Used by permission NavPress Publishing Group.

Cover and Interior Design by Camille Green

Darlene Photograph by David Anderson Photography

Printed by Emerald Press, Sydney, Australia

ISBN 978-0-9806499-0-1

THIS BOOK IS DEDICATED TO
MY OWN CHILDREN,
AMY, CHLOE AND ZOE JEWEL,
WHOSE LIVES INSPIRE ME TO LIVE
WITH JOY AND PURPOSE,
THEIR FUTURE MY GREATEST MOTIVATOR,
THEIR 'DREAMS COME TRUE'
MY GREATEST PRAYER.

EPHESIANS 5:1-2
WATCH WHAT GOD DOES, AND THEN DO
IT, LIKE CHILDREN WHO LEARN PROPER
BEHAVIOUR FROM THEIR PARENTS. MOSTLY
WHAT GOD DOES IS LOVE YOU. KEEP
COMPANY WITH HIM AND LEARN A LIFE
OF LOVE. OBSERVE HOW CHRIST LOVED
US. HIS LOVE WAS NOT CAUTIOUS BUT
EXTRAVAGANT. HE DID NOT LOVE IN ORDER
TO GET SOMETHING FROM US BUT TO GIVE
EVERYTHING OF HIMSELF TO US.
LOVE LIKE THAT.

THE MESSAGE

the great generational transition

FOREWORD BY: JACK HAYFORD

IT IS ALWAYS significant when someone fully in touch with the Church globally speaks into the present moment.

Darlene Zschech is such a person, and thankfully she is intensely practical.

Darlene is not only an influencer of the Global Church worship life through her music and gifting, she is an experienced pastoral leader, and a respected voice to today's youth culture. Further, she is a faithful wife and an effective mother; she and her husband Mark have 3 children, aged 20, 17 and 8.

So it is without reserve, in this book you have in hand workable wisdom from a lady who is qualified to be heard by all of us.

My respect for the writer transcends her remarkable personal gifts. It is prompted by the clear-headedness, the Word-centredness and Christ-consciousness that she evidences.

Whether you encounter her as a worship leader, hear her as an internationally welcomed speaker, or if you've conversed with her as I often have as a friend, you encounter genuine sincerity, spiritual substance and personal graciousness.

I've listed the above six qualities about Darlene, not only because they're true of her but because they are so necessary to each of us today. They are values that must be relayed and reinforced — traits needful of transmission to a rising generation by mentors and models living them as they help serve and shape the younger ones watching and following us.

I think you'll find "fresh air" within these pages — a breath of insight and inspiration to increase our sensitivities and response to these remarkable times.

Societal change is so rapid, confusion and deception are a constant threat unless balance and weight are added by those with discerning perspective. That's why I'm thankful for the content here. It will help each of us to perceive and address the moment — adding balance and weight to our own experience, enriching our own potential for investing it in those we are called by God to help rise to their own life-purpose.

So, as you begin, let me urge you to join me in responding to its message. Whether you're a part of the rising generation itself, or one of the host of us called to welcome and assist them to their potential to make an eternal difference in our world, join with me.

Let's tune to the times being addressed by this prophetic message at this pivotal moment.

The message is clear: It's ours to hear.

And to take action — now!

Jack W. Hayford

Founding Pastor, The Church on the Way
Founder-Chancellor, The King's Seminary
President, Foursquare Church International

the great generational transition

INTRODUCTION: THE WHY AND THE WHAT

INTRODUCTION ... A good place to start.

Psalm 145:3-7, 'God is magnificent; He can never be praised enough. There are no boundaries to His greatness. Generation after generation stands in awe of Your work; each one tells stories of Your mighty acts. Your beauty and splendour have everyone talking; I compose songs on Your wonders. Your marvellous doings are headline news; I could write a book full of the details of Your greatness. The fame of Your goodness spreads across the country; Your righteousness is on everyone's lips.' (The Message)

If the title of this leadership handbook sounds a bit like an adventure book, then my friend, you are right on track!

This stage of my story in ministry has been one of the greatest adventures ever... including some of the hardest moments, but by far some of the sweetest.

I have endeavoured to write as practically as I can, with honest and realistic answers to some of the hurdles presented over time and, by the grace of God, I pray you are equipped to walk into this season with kindness and great strength.

Mark and I and our family are honoured to be part of a great local church for many years, Hillsong Church in Sydney Australia, where leadership is modelled and encouraged, and where bringing through the next generation has always been one of the priorities and strategies that remain of high importance.

This is my frame of reference... doing life in a team of leaders, leading a highly creative team whose life passion is to go on the ride of discovering what worship truly means, personally working hard to develop my own leadership abilities, sitting under great leadership, reading, reading and more reading... and listening, observing and chatting with many leaders I have had the privilege of getting to know.

And this is what I know to be true... that if life was merely about our own sense of personal fulfilment, then I guess many of the words in this book would be unnecessary – BUT if you follow the great example of Jesus Christ, who came and lived and died for people, and if we are saved by His grace and changed to love like He loves... then we gain a little more insight into what is valuable in the economy of the Kingdom of God. A life lived IN Christ is a sacrificial life, a life poured out, a life lived to lift the lives of

OTHERS.

From the moment I stepped into my local church as a very tender 15-year-old, there was definitely that feeling of 'coming home'. And this open-armed welcome was actually one of the divine things about the house of God which I have always loved, and as I've grown and become more familiar with what His house and His people represent... well, I have come to value and appreciate the presence of God in His sons and daughters in a completely sacred and tender way.

And I guess due to my own journey as a disciple of Christ, who was always willing in heart, but very broken in soul... is one of the reasons I am so passionate about seeing this generation, and the generations to come, brought through into a strong and powerful understanding of who each of us are in Christ... and how valuable and needed every one of us is RIGHT NOW.

But in saying all that, as I've journeyed through church life, I have definitely seen that the great divide has well and truly existed when it comes to one generation even being AWARE of the next, let alone there being a whole hearted commitment to raising up and encouraging new ways and fresh ideas from those who may be decades younger, but have an outstanding dedication to the things of God. So this book does not serve to say to anyone feeling older or out of date that your time is over, time to stand aside.

On the contrary, this book is written to give you tools to empower those God has entrusted to you to mentor and inspire, AND then to give you a little bit of well worn info that just might save you a whole lot of heartache in the future!!

And as you will find along the way, as you pour yourself into seeing other people's dreams come true, the Lord has an amazing way of continuing to bring to pass some of those unrealised dreams in your own life.

'Delight yourself in the Lord, and He will give you the desires of your heart...'
Psalm 37:4.

A couple of years ago, I had the awesome opportunity to sit and have coffee with the great leadership teacher, John Maxwell, and as he has had a major influence in my life, I was like a sponge to all he had to say. But I had come with a specific question as to raising strong leadership generationally, I wanted to hear his heart on the matter, and glean from his experience in areas of family, ministry, and in business... as to how this strength we are experiencing can be sustained. He looked at me and said,

'that unless the WHY behind the WHAT is taught consistently, that unless we preach a standard and not just a method, then yes, clarity, precision, and most importantly, the original WHY becomes very distorted amidst all the DOING.'

I just listened intently and wrote as fast as my little hand would go, and asked God for wisdom AND great grace for this next season.

And even though I still have much to learn in so many areas of life, I do know for sure that this generation of worshippers and leaders coming through want to be involved with message and music that move people to the core of their being, that move people to respond... that confront us to change, and MOST importantly, message and music that welcome the Holy Spirit in power and might, filled with authentic experience and lyrics that have been tested in the fire and morphed from simply imagination, to anthems of faith!

They are not interested in giving their lives to passive, plastic melodies or simply a method of worship or a particular style of life that seems to work.

For once you've tasted the reality of the presence of God, not just hype or excitement, but the great filling of His glory through your veins, well, your spiritual taste buds are simply ruined for anything counterfeit.

There is NO substitute for His presence, for in His presence we are changed, AND... we behold His glory.

Nothing ever can or ever will compare... for how can we encounter God Himself and remain the same?

I have endeavoured to keep this book as strong and practical as I can, so rather than chapters, I have titled each section as a VALUE, as I have found that each of these topics are critical to prepare the ground for any successful shift, whether it is large or small. They are in no particular order, and I am sure there will be values that apply to your situation more aptly than others.

I pray that as you read and consider these thoughts, you'll consider how Psalm 145 could come to pass in your own day-to-day environment... that your personal sense and commitment to what could be possible in your lifetime would be fuelled and encouraged.

Whether you live in countries that are in early development stages or countries that have more access to funding and opportunity, whether you are a part of a local church that is embracing change or one that is resisting on all sides, or in your own personal circumstance there is a lot of change going on, all I know is that the Word of God works WHEREVER it is applied.

Let's go on this journey... I SO believe in you.

Darlene.

the great generational transition

VALUE ONE: TIME FOR GROWTH

ZECHARIAH 8:4
A MESSAGE FROM GOD-OF-THE-ANGEL-
ARMIES: 'OLD MEN AND OLD WOMEN
WILL COME BACK TO JERUSALEM, SIT ON
BENCHES ON THE STREETS AND SPIN TALES,
MOVE AROUND SAFELY WITH THEIR CANES—A
GOOD CITY TO GROW OLD IN. AND BOYS
AND GIRLS WILL FILL THE PUBLIC PARKS,
LAUGHING AND PLAYING—A GOOD CITY TO
GROW UP IN.'

THE MESSAGE

IN ANY SEASON where transition is required, there is a growth phase that is critical to the transitor AND the transitee.

Growth is necessary for all of us, and you can be guaranteed that there will always be growing pains associated with stretch and change. But take heart, growing pains are normal! All of the great things in life take time and patience and discomfort to achieve all they were intended for.

You see the words 'HOW LONG?' printed often in the Psalms, as the psalmist cries out to heaven.

'How long do I have to wait until the hand of God steps into my reality and brings about the miracle that only He can supply?'

I am sure most of you reading have prayed prayers asking for intervention, pleading your case during some sort of character building season in your life…

How long until this situation will turn around? How long until those questions in my heart will be answered? How long until someone actually HEARS me rather than just dismisses me?

The list goes on and on.

How long, I have prayed so many times, will it take for us as leaders and friends to realise that it is our responsibility to pass on what we know, and to empower those coming behind us, whether it be our own natural children, or those in our sphere that we lead and influence?

I am crazy enough to even think that we can become part of the great global revolution within the body of Christ and actually have a dynamic part to play.

There is a definite shift in the atmosphere, there is a stirring in the hearts of so many to see change and to have some sort of influence in how that change evolves – possible??

In my heart of hearts I believe it is SO possible.

I DO know for sure, that we are living in times that those who have gone before us diligently dreamed about, prayed about and bravely pioneered, and that the level of unity across the body of Christ is increasing, that the Spirit-fuelled passion to relieve human suffering is building in intensity and efficiency throughout the earth.

So yes, faith is rising and HOPE remains strong even though the state of humanity is in dire need, and the church, as beautiful as she is, is GROWING in her under-standing and confidence of who she needs to be.

But the great news is that the generations are getting stronger. The revelation of God's plan and purpose on the earth is bringing to bloom even the hardest of hearts… and these are amazing days to be found in.

Psalm 78, in verse 7 says that 'each generation should put its hope anew in God, not forgetting His glorious miracles and obeying His commands'.

Verse 8 says, 'Then, they will not be like their ancestors – stubborn, rebellious, and unfaithful, refusing to give their hearts to God'.

These are such strategic days, to live each of our season cycles well is SO critical to the continued succession of what could be the greatest revolution of human hearts in history!

Within this season we have also seen emerge a great arena of extremely CONFIDENT young men and woman, people who have been captivated by the awesome love of God at an early age, and are seriously ready to lay it all down for the sake of Christ.

Now, that means that we end up LEADING such an array of amazing people, older and younger, highly ambitious, extremely talented, opinionated, success-ful, passionate, talented, undisciplined, some just with less obvious talents, many fatherless kids (which means their sense of boundaries is often non-existent) and personally, as a leader, I have had to GROW in my capacity to lead on every level.

Many of the leadership subjects we have found needed to be taught within our home context of worship team within church life have ended up having very little to do with music, but MUCH to do with discipleship and simply learning about the heart of God toward us.

And as most great opportunities don't look like great opportunities when they are first presented to you as problems, I have honestly and continuously asked God for wisdom every day in order to lead well.

Wow, what a journey....

We find continually throughout the Psalms, that there is a specific revealed truth mentioned many times, about declaring the faithfulness of God to the next generation, and actually taking it on as a responsibility rather than simply a nice idea or romantic notion.

In Psalm 71, we find David asking God to continue to give him breath until he has adequately told of His greatness and power to the next generation.

And in Psalm 145, one of my life's signature chapters where God continues to speak to me and challenge me from, here we find David again, prophetically singing over the future generations, describing what we are a part of today and what has been gathering momentum for hundreds and hundreds of years... generations being absolutely devoted and captivated by the glorious nature of our King.

Verse 18 says, 'Lord, Yes, even when I am old and grey, O God forsake me not, but keep me alive until I have declared Your mighty strength to this generation, and Your might and power to all that are to come'. (AMP)

Just like in David's day, there is much talk about mentoring, and bringing through the next generation, AND a lot of it sounds so very wonderful. But the truth of the matter is, that to bring through the next generation well takes courageous leaders who are willing to give away their knowledge and understanding for the Kingdom's sake.

It sounds easy, but within church history, you'll find many times where this was not done in a good way at all, and the next generation was not brought through well...

And God has had to wait again for people to rise and be strong and faithful with all He has entrusted to us, including the development and shepherding of new generations who are ready to proclaim the gospel with their own sound and approach.

In Deuteronomy 1 & 2, we hear about a struggle between Moses, the Israelites, and the will of God... and God Himself having to wait 38 years until an entire generation had passed away, so His perfect will could be seen.

This was a generation who, under Moses' leadership, was seeing just incredible favour from the hand of God.

God went before them, sending even a fire by night and a cloud by day to show them the way to get to all that was purposed for them. But rebellion, stubborn hearts, disobedience and just people acting on a 'hunch' that they knew better than God did became their undoing.

The Lord Himself ends up saying to Moses in Deuteronomy 1:34 that, 'Not a man of this evil generation shall see the good land which I swore to your forefathers except for Caleb... he will see it, and I will give it to him and his descendants, because he has followed the Lord wholeheartedly'.

You know, the disappointment you feel as a parent at times when your children deliberately choose to be disobedient, is very real and something that you wrestle with.

WE are racked with those questions and doubts.

'Where have I gone wrong? Why aren't they listening? Why don't they see that their actions will result in a much harsher outcome?' etc, etc.

I do wonder at times how our God, who sees the beginning from the end, and is all knowing and all powerful, must feel when we stray due to our own hasty decisions, pride, ignorance and a lack of understanding of the greater picture.

The real hero however in this Deuteronomy story is Moses, who as a leader, just keeps on keeping on... leading and directing those who would listen, and in

Deuteronomy 4, he says to them as a caution and reminder, 'The Lord your God destroyed from among you everyone who followed the Baal of Peor, but all of you who held fast to the Lord your God are still alive today... see, I have taught you decrees and laws as the Lord my God has commanded me, so that you may follow them in the land you are entering to take possession of it...'

'Teach them to your children, and to their children'.

The scriptures that follow are some of the most powerful teaching on obedience and sacrifice – and then the ten commandments are laid out for all of us.

When the principles of WHY we do certain things are not taught well, the effectiveness of the outcome eventually wears down as people follow a system out of routine to achieve results rather than live out of their convictions.

The problem in communicating and teaching life principles effectively was highlighted a few years ago in WORTH Magazine, and it made the comparison, stressing the struggle of handing down generational finance so that responsibility and understanding were also handed on.

Needless to say, SO many times when it comes to simply handing down financial wealth to those who have not had to earn it themselves is a great challenge.

It was noted, and I quote, 'By and large, inheritors of wealth have no appreciation of what is required to build it. The theory is that the first generation starts off in a rice paddy, meaning two people with an affinity for one another come together and create a financial fortune... the second generation moves to the city, puts on beautiful clothes, joins the opera board, runs big organisations, and the fortune plateaus. The third generation, with no experience of work, consumes the financial fortune, and the fourth generation goes back to the rice paddy'.[1]

For some of you reading you might see this as an example that really doesn't feel like it applies, EXCEPT, when the why we do what we do doesn't permeate in all we do, the truth of the value systems are compromised simply because of unsuccessful strategy when sharing our knowledge, vision and passions BEHIND whatever it is we do and whoever it is we are.

And that's where we, as spiritual mums and dads, need to lay hold of the wonderful privilege we have in passing down knowledge, passing down experience, example, and passing down such a rich legacy of faith that those the Lord is preparing to stand strong at the frontline will always be able to bring personal, challenging, yet faithful miracle stories to mind, to know that if God could do it then, He can do it now.

But in this day and age, we are not very good at taking the time to sit and converse at levels needed to exchange truths, OR, we are not very good at taking the time to listen to those who have been forging the path ahead of us.

Without appropriate teaching of a hands-on experience, and may I say, without a personal revelation, then taking what is handed to you and making it stronger is very difficult.

Another great historical example of this was when it came to some of the music of the church.

Before the times of Handel and Bach, much of church music was really in the hands of ordinary churchman as in those days, the only people in a town who were known to have any education and culture were found in the church.

It was through St Ambrose, Archbishop of Milan from 374–397, who took a keen interest in the music that was being introduced as prayers and worship in the church. He devised a special form of chanting, known from his name, as the Ambrosian chant. This really developed a new song from within the walls of many a house of worship, but when Ambrose died, church music in his sphere of influence died as well.

Great for a season, but without generational revelation, the great baton passing never really took place.

It took another 200 years before Pope Gregory brought about a new method of song in the house of God, and thus the 'Gregorian Chant' was born, and due to its reason and method being taught to others much younger, it is still alive and well today.

Actually, if you ever get the opportunity to stand in one of the grand cathedrals to hear this song being proclaimed… rather than judge it, close your eyes and think about the greatness of our God, and the sacrifice of so many who have gone before, and allow your heart to be moved in a spectacular way.

I am so very aware of the responsibility and great honour we have of inspiring and teaching those coming behind us, and I am also very aware that in my own personal sphere of influence, that my platform, that is the platform of influence that God has given me, is actually their starting point!

So, we must never just teach a method or a 'rote' way of serving or living, but a biblically rich understanding of WHY we do WHAT we do! – for we know that without vision, people perish… but guess what, with vision and understanding they flourish!!

People want something to live for and to die for.

We need to teach those coming through that what they are involved with is HOLY, that developing your life of worship is critical to a devoted life in every believer.

In the book of Acts 10:15 it says, 'Do not treat that which is Holy (pure) as if it were common'. (AMP)

This is a very significant scripture – and one I like to take time to think about as it surely keeps bland living as a Christ follower at a safe distance – especially as our heart and its health determines where we find ourselves.

How easy is it to do though, especially when you get a bit familiar with either your current platform, or the people around you, or even the presence of God Himself.

In Matthew 7:6 in the Message translation it says, 'Don't be flip with the sacred. Banter and silliness give no honour to God. Don't reduce Holy mysteries to slogans. In trying to be relevant, you're only being cute and inviting sacrilege.'

The time is NOW my friends to pick up all that is in your heart and dust it off, even if you've had some disappointments along the way. Take a deep breath and simply get moving in the lane you KNOW is waiting for you to run in, whether you are training others, or whether you are just starting to take your first steps toward your heart's desire.

Here we go… making history is all about these defining moments setting us alight on the inside… and then actually getting about and doing it!

Everywhere you look there are young men and women with great skill, creativity, passion and ideas, who with someone like you or I to believe in them and support them, or simply take the time to let them speak about their dreams, well, this is the beginning of seeing greatness and potential realised.

If there is one thing I've learned about parenting with my own children, it's that the time you spend just one-on-one with them and hearing your kids speak about the things they daydream about, this is where you get to the real heartbeat of your child.

There is no substitute for time or having open ears to hear.

Valuable, precious time….

There is a couple in our own church who are extremely busy people, they are older than us, with grown children… they run a successful business and advise many others on business, and they have the most incredible hearts after God.

But what Mark and I love about this couple the most is that at least once a year or more they will take the time and INSIST we have a meal together, and they will talk to us about where we are at, how our children are, the health of our hearts, etc, etc, and they take the TIME to mentor, to inspire, and to simply love.

You cannot put a dollar value on how much this means to Mark and I, and to have someone looking out for us on our journey in life. We all have the ability to be generous with our time toward those looking for leadership and the right way to live life.

Let's be committed to growth, even though it mostly means change.

Without it, we become very old, very quickly.

Honour all that has been, but LEAN into all that is to come.

Our deepest fear is not that we are inadequate. Our deepest fear is that we are powerful beyond measure. It is our light, not our darkness that most frightens us. Your playing small does not serve the world. There is nothing enlightened about shrinking so that other people won't feel insecure around you. We are all meant to shine as children do. It's not just in some of us, it's in everyone. And as we let our own lights shine, we unconsciously give other people permission to do the same. As we are liberated from our own fear, our presence automatically liberates others.[2]

Marianne Williamson

the great generational transition

VALUE TWO: ENCOURAGEMENT

HEBREWS 10:25
LET US NOT GIVE UP
MEETING TOGETHER, AS SOME ARE
IN THE HABIT OF DOING, BUT LET US
ENCOURAGE ONE ANOTHER,
AND ALL THE MORE AS YOU SEE THE
DAY APPROACHING.

NIV

TIME GOES BY so very fast.

I find it so hard to fathom that my own first born daughter is now a married woman, building her future with the man of her dreams… sometimes a week can fly by so quickly it takes you by surprise when you find yourself back at Sunday again!!

But with this in mind, we must be continually aware of the urgency and value of preparing not just the next generation, but speaking life and potential into the third and fourth.

I will never forget a dear Pastor friend of ours, Ps Rick Godwin from San Antonio, Texas saying to me, 'Darlene, the two greatest days of your life are the day you were born, and the day you found out why.'

These words just resonated so very deep within me, as my clear memory of feeling a sense of being 'set apart' for Kingdom endeavour was definitely a time in my life where literally the lights went on for me deep in my spirit. You find throughout history that all of the truly great men and women were committed to speaking direction and promise into the lives of those around them, and this is something every one of us can eventually make part of 'who we are', rather than another job we have to do.

I personally have many memories of my parents, grandparents, church leaders and friends filling my soul with encouragement, when I did not have the courage myself to believe in the dreams that were already filling my heart.

I have learned that for many of us, and many of the great men and women around us, it is a rare day when support is received that would breathe life into the dreams and hopes we cling to and sincerely believe in.

Following the example of our God when it comes to encouragement is premium.

Psalm 10:16 says, 'The Lord is King forever and ever; the nations will perish from His land. You hear O Lord, the desire of the afflicted; You encourage them, and You listen to their cry, defending the Fatherless and the oppressed in order that man, who is of the earth, may terrify no more.'

There are many times in our every day where we can find ourselves genuinely encouraged from moments that are not based solely on others.

I am encouraged in my soul when I hear good music, I am encouraged when I see an amazing garden or piece of art, I am encouraged when I hear a great message being preached, I am encouraged when I see my family doing life well and working together well.

I am encouraged when I see my husband reading and studying the Word, I am encouraged when I read about someone going against all odds and succeeding in life.

Yes, there are many, many moments if you choose to see them, that will be a part of giving you strength, even in the fleeting moments. I get encouraged,

ESPECIALLY when music is created that gives glory to God... hearing orchestras playing melodies that were written to express the grandeur of the King of Kings.

Oh, I feel encouraged just writing about it.

What is it that encourages you?

I asked a close girlfriend of mine that question the other day as she was feeling so low, and she could not find her answer.

I tapped into the emotional capacity of music very early, and I would find that certain songs with uplifting messages would encourage me even when there was no one physically around to do this.

One of the reasons for having music such as praise and worship playing in our homes and cars is that you start to see music do what it was created to do, as the Word of Life fills the atmosphere, the human spirit is lifted again.

The language of music has always fascinated me... created to carry the presence of God, created to give voice to the human journey, created as a vehicle of expression of the human heart and often communicating a far deeper level of speech than words alone can ever express. Created to communicate the cries, the anguish, the joys, the highs and the lows. David says in Psalm 71, 'When I open up in song to You, I let out lungsful of praise, my rescued life a song.'! (The Message) I wish I could tell you how much I love that verse.

On my journey as a young woman discovering what ministry truly meant and required, I cannot tell you how many times people would try and bring me back to earth, so to speak, when I would tell them of my purpose and intent. I was young and full of enthusiasm, full of passion for music and hungry for knowledge about worship... BUT so many around me would try to dissuade me in my ministry goals so I would not get my hopes up for fear of facing disappointment.

I wondered for many years why people felt the need to try to 'small me' down.

Psalm 139:17, 'How precious and weighty also are Your thoughts toward me O God. How vast is the sum of them.'

Verse 18, 'If I could count them, they would be more in number than the sand... When I awoke (could I count to the end) I would still be with You.' (AMP)

In our own church environment in Sydney, Australia, and I gather in most of the planet, rather than finding multitudes who think more highly of themselves, I have honestly found that the opposite is true... that there are so, so, so many people who honestly think more lowly of themselves. But it doesn't take much of a language shift to ensure that what we bring to the lives of those around us on a consistent level is the power of acceptance and support.

I have never seen such a simple strategy have such brilliant impact!!

EVERY SINGLE PERSON NEEDS TO KNOW THEY ARE VALUED AND COMPLETELY VALUABLE.

Psalm 45 is the Psalm that the Holy Spirit wrote across the fabric of my being for three whole days and nights when my Pastor asked me to take on the worship department of our church. We took our little family off to the beach for a mini holiday to talk and pray about what this would mean. I was simply overwhelmed with all the things I didn't know about this new role, with all the inadequacies I knew about myself and felt would be enough to drown me AND take others down with me! But I stood at the edge of the ocean early one morning and really felt that God was saying I could choose, and whichever way I went, He would give me wisdom, moment by moment, and grace for each day.

Toward the end of Psalm 45 it says, 'and your sons will take the place of your fathers, you will make them princes throughout the land'.

To be honest, at the time it made NO sense to me, but as the years have evolved and my heart has become more refined and secure with the message of releasing others… well, now it definitely makes sense and reveals to me again God's heart for succession and multiplication, releasing the sons and the daughters… to see them as the planting of the Lord, in every corner of the globe. Completely stunning!!

And as for the daughters, don't EVER lose heart and think God could not use you - of course He will.

God made both man and woman, humankind (or kind humans), different but equal, to have dominion, made in His image…

Oh, and what a great idea!!

I have friends who work tirelessly throughout India feeding, teaching and believing in a seemingly forgotten generation. To watch their strategy with the young women to whom often basic education is not even an option (just on this, EVERY person should have access to education – let's change this!!!), well, the encouragement strategy has literally changed a hopeless atmosphere to one of grand possibility time and time again.

The results they have seen simply through filling an atmosphere with praise and life and GENUINE encouragement, even when this has never been the prevailing culture, has brought about truly stunning outcomes. Where possibility reigns, life breeds life. An outstanding God principle!!

You may look around and it may not be immediately evident to you who you could pour your life into, but I would suggest that you just start with the first one you see, younger or older. It is outstanding to see the possibility in someone start to rise once they know and understand that they are loved and appreciated and have a life that is worth showing up for.

I think that on the earth today there are many places where there certainly has been a shift from a prevailing language of negativity, to a culture of hard work and possibility and that in many places you visit, you will sense an atmosphere of

'whatever it takes, we will do it!'

A fantastic banner to have over your life, and one made very famous by Mother Teresa who was renowned for taking just whatever was in her hand, and turning it into whatever the need required.

But another great way to live and take this idea further into a 'releasing others' framework is ... hey, 'whatever it takes...YOU can do it!!'

Not out of 'passing the buck', but seriously, if every initiative in my own world had to come from me or be outworked by me, we would be in serious trouble!!

Empowering others is the key here.

And once you start to share the workload AND the responsibility, AND the credit, well, you light a fire deep on the inside of others, giving them experience and helping them to work out what on earth it is they are even good at. Encouragement is a truly powerful force and when it is done sincerely and often, the creative dynamic within the act of encouraging someone over a lifetime has the ability to see the seemingly ordinary rise to become more than they could have ever imagined.

There is a powerful lyric found within the Delirious song, OUR GOD REIGNS that says, 'He's a Father who loves to parade you' – it gets me every time.[3]

Imagine that?

That God who created the heavens and the earth actually gets a kick out of every one of us!

I know the pride and the swelled chest that became my husband's stance after the birth of our first daughter, Amy Jaye. After she was born, he and my mum finally went home after no sleep that night, and they stayed up ALL the next night as well while Mark talked about just how beautiful and perfect and divine and lovely beyond words Amy was (and is!!). The heart of our heavenly Father is even SO much more besotted by each of us, that He gave His son to ensure our salvation.

That's a crazy, out of this world kind of love.

There have been countless times however that I have seen a crippled sense of self worth overcome so many, causing their expressive hearts to become misguided and lied to. When passion for life is disillusioned, it will often erupt in areas of anger and resentment, or simply result in lives being minimised merely to fit in or be accepted, living way below God's intended purpose.

My prayer is that our willingness to encourage would be fuelled by an agenda that is clean, and motivated by love.

An unselfish, unspoiled, generous-hearted LOVE.

For it is in the knowing that you are loved that gives voice to a Holy assurance in our lives.

The atmosphere and grossly misled worth systems of our world can so easily stuff the wrong values down our throats, so that if you are not wealthy, well known, if you don't feel beautiful enough or thin enough, accepted enough, or even normal enough, if your friends are not in the IN crowd etc, then the courageous person you KNOW is inside feels so inferior, that it seems easier to stay small than to go against the tide of our culture. Or if those in your immediate surroundings are saying 'you'll never amount to anything, who do you think you are?' etc, etc, that is one heck of an atmosphere to have to continually rise above.

But words carry life.

Proverbs 15:4. 'The soothing tongue is a tree of life, but a perverse tongue crushes the spirit.'

This is exactly what happens - when a spirit is crushed, so is the emotional energy required to see potential released, but when the words coming from you are filled with support, the tree of life is at its finest work to bring forth beautiful fruit.

I personally spent most of my childhood SO internally struggling with the torment of insecurity, that the effects of that almost caused my own body to shut down due to a bulimic lifestyle, and a continuously troubled spirit that seemed to overwhelm my naturally happy heart.

I grew up singing, grew up being encouraged by a mum who thought the sun shone out from me (she still does, that's a mothers love!!), but despite it all, it was as if the enemy himself would try to tear my soul apart. Aside from my own family who tried their best to console me, there were two women in my local church, Beth and Desley, who literally came alongside me, accepted me, encouraged me, welcomed me into their homes, who happened to be the leaders of the music department (how lovely is God to set that up!!), and loved me amidst all my tender-hearted but very misguided baggage.

I am ever grateful to them for loving and inspiring me as they did...

Cheering me on in my dreams, encouraging me in my areas of gifting, but more importantly, showing me the way to God.

What I do see in the Bible, is that it appears that children and infants, just young but filled with God-designed purpose and potential, have always been targeted by the enemy to see their lives cut short BEFORE they learn for themselves that the name of Jesus is greater than any trial. Psalm 8 declares the power that is released from the mouths and hearts of praising children as they literally SILENCE the enemy with their own stance of faith.

I remember one day, many years ago now, when one of our incredible worship leaders who was only young, was meant to be leading a service... and he was nowhere to be seen at the venue where we were rehearsing, even though I knew

I had seen his car. I went outside and started looking as I sensed that something was not quite right. I followed my instinct, and sure enough, there he was, sitting in the gutter on the side of the car park, just staring into space.

After a little while of chatting, he started to open up to me and say that he felt that as a leader, he just did not have what it took.

It was at a period of time when a few well known ministers around the world had made foolish choices, and as a young man of God, this guy who suddenly faces the fact that some of his mentors had fallen, well, my young friend said that he had NO right to lead anybody if this was the only way forward. I felt so sad that day, and wished I could take his disillusioned heart and just put it all the right way up for him. But what I did discover was that the simple but powerful way of encouragement was enough to put a young man back on his feet, and by the grace of God he is well and truly on his feet today. He's now one of the finest worship leaders and writers that I know, generous to the core, and so tender-hearted toward broken humanity that his life is a great inspiration personally to Mark and I, and I know to countless others.

Encouraging words, fuelled by the Word of God which is ALIVE, is like a cold drink of the finest water to the desperately thirsty soul.

There are so many great, small but significant things you can do practically to encourage others.

Just a simple thing like saying, 'that was wonderful! well done!' can take that moment of 'I hope this was OK' and turn it around to breathe a quiet assurance in the hearer's heart.

In my specific area of training up new leaders of worship - or if there is a leader feeling particularly vulnerable at a certain time - just a simple thing I do ON PURPOSE is to stand where they can see me from the corner of their eye, and my role in that moment is to simply cheer them on, even if you simply are like a bit of a security blanket, just being aware to give encouragement, staying inconspicuous, not letting anyone else know that is what you are doing and simply setting them up to win. The feedback we receive from little practical moments like this is incredible.

Talking through mistakes or musical 'train wrecks' also helps to keep any kind of faults in their place, and helping those coming through to see that if an error was made, that it was simply a bad musical choice, rather than anything to do with their character.

It is a very insecure, manipulative leader who will take your character to task over a simple, innocent mistake.

Over the years, I have seen literally hundreds of men and woman leave churches or ministry over events and mistakes on a platform such as these, that were not handled lovingly but simply either unspoken of, and then they were never used again, or they were berated publicly only to be lost in a sea of humiliation. A lot of what we do is in a public arena, so you find there is less room for error and certainly nowhere to hide when you make a blunder.

Encouragement is welcomed at any time, but it is CRITICAL to those in stages of early development, or to those who have just simply made an error and are feeling emotionally fragile.

And I might add, developing ON PURPOSE your sense of humour will certainly make moments like these (and many others) much easier to cope with!!

I personally have made so many mistakes while leading worship, or speaking, not to mention all the countless mistakes I've made OFF the platform. You learn over time that if you don't laugh at yourself, AND be kind to yourself when you've made an innocent mistake, that life would certainly be SO much harder to negotiate.

Encouragement is also a superb act of kindness, as it puts those you encourage on a wonderful, lifted atmosphere – an atmosphere of LIFE and promise, rather than simply settling for the atmosphere of status quo.

And kindness is infectious.

When facing personality conflicts, even insecurity issues, it's incredible how a stance of kindness offered to those around you tends to release a fragrance of selflessness, often putting your own issues at bay.

Generosity is also another stance you should adopt as again, the encouragement received from a simple act of generosity is far-reaching and definitely stirs greatness in a spiritual realm.

I was recently admiring one of the young musician's new guitar, it was incredible, and very expensive I might add. He was treating it like it was his own child, and it obviously meant a lot to him. I made a comment to him that he must have worked and saved hard for it, but with tears in his eyes he told me about one of the other guys in the team who simply gave him this guitar, as a way to encourage him in his deep desire to play and write songs that would truly grip the human soul… a beautiful, costly act of generosity, that resourced a stunning moment of encouragement that will leave a lasting legacy.

I have a very dear friend who years ago, through simply praying God's will for her life, ended up receiving an instruction from heaven that found her calling me one day to say that she had a gift for me and needed me to receive it ASAP!

I was quite intrigued, and could not believe it when she told me that she needed to give me her grand piano. I was shocked, and so, so excited, as I had been praying for a piano that I could write and worship from (I DID NOT ask for a grand, and am still very humbled by this act of generosity).

I SO did not expect an extravagant gift like this, but WOW, the encouragement I received that day and to this!

That piano sits in the middle of our lounge room today, it is in the heart of our home, and every time I see it, play it, hear my children play it, I am so inspired that the God of heaven and earth heard my simple prayers and honoured them, AND heard my girlfriend's prayers and honoured her with SO much more than a piano. You see, encouragement is active, not passive, and SO illuminating for both the giver and the receiver.

1 Cor 8:1, 'Yet mere knowledge causes people to be puffed up (to bear themselves loftily and to be proud), but LOVE, (affection and goodwill and benevolence) edifies and builds up and encourages one to grow to his full stature.' (AMP)

One of the most encouraging pastors that I have ever had the privilege to meet is Pastor Tommy Barnett from Phoenix First Assembly in Phoenix USA. As church Pastor and church planter and Founder of the Dream Centre, his own church is known as 'The Church with a Heart', and its reputation is well earned.

Joyce Meyer always says that apart from her husband, if there was one extra person who she would love to have travel with her all the time it would be Pastor Tommy, because of his ability to ENCOURAGE.

He has stood in many a meeting as I have led the worship, and afterward will come up and just pour words of life out over you, literally leaving you feeling like you could do anything! And the amazing thing is, he lives like this everyday... to every person he meets, his children, his staff, those he personally leads, those he mentors. He does not reserve his encouraging words for Sundays or for those who could reciprocate with favours. No, this man's life is defined through encouragement. I actually asked him a couple of questions about raising up another generation and these were his answers:

What would you say was your greatest joy in ministry?

Seeing my children serving God and all three working with me in the ministry!

What would be your biggest frustration when training younger ministers?

Wanting it all NOW! Not enjoying the "journey".

What would be the ONE THING you would want a younger pastor/ leader to take into his future in serving God?

That living a righteous life is the number one priority. Because righteousness and provision for the vision go together. "Seek first the kingdom of God and all these other things will be added."

In your opinion, what would be the main obstacle that takes young men and women out of the ministry?

Discouragement! And they give up too quickly!

With your own children, what has been the most important value you have shown them in life as far as serving God and all that this means?

Keep your eyes on God and then the God-given vision for their lives. Men at best are just men. But GOD never fails!!!

Thanks Pastor Tommy.

Where there has been a huge lack of encouraging words spoken over you in your lifetime, you need to learn how to

BUILD YOURSELF UP

with the Word of God, and not just wait for everyone else to come and lift your spirits. Even if you are in a tough or dry kind of season in life,

STIR YOURSELF UP.

Position words of life wherever you spend time, so that even if you don't FEEL like getting happy, you cannot avoid it.

One of my dear girlfriends who lost her first child surrounded herself with scripture and promise, and played loud worship music until the neighbours almost moved out!! She didn't FEEL like reading words of life, but was obedient to the Word of God anyway, and we all watched as the heart of this great woman was tended to oh so carefully by the Master Shepherd Himself... and she has emerged with grace and dignity, just as the Bible declares.

On one of my husband's first trips into East Africa, he met with a whole lot of pastors and leaders from different denominations, and many of the local government representatives. They were all discussing the varied ways that we in the west could be of most benefit to their land, how best we could serve the people. There were many great ideas, and need that was both immediate and long term. Mark was fuelled with grass roots, real conversation that would empower us to do the best with the resource we had available.

The ONE question however that he was unprepared for was when they were discussing the youth and some of the challenges they faced, and the enquiry from the leader of youth came as this.

'Can you teach us how to think??'

Mark was floored, as what this particular minister went on to explain was that even if many millions of dollars were poured into the land today, they felt that the correct procedure and energy and creative wisdom needed to facilitate that kind of gift was not encouraged or found amongst the youth who are the leaders of tomorrow.

Actually, what we discovered in many of these developing nations is something known as IDLE, a greater epidemic than HIV/AIDS or malaria.

Through a high state of unemployment, lack of education opportunities, no encouragement when it comes to dreams, and often just very little money available to support any ambition, a state of being IDLE every day has been perpetuated.

Nowhere to go, nothing to do, don't dream for the risk of you being disappointed is too high, so best just live as part of the status quo.

There are people living all over the world in varied states of war, poverty, disease, hunger and ruin, and even the fact that they still get up in the morning when able is a miracle to me. Ahhhh, but such is the resilience of the human spirit, for when God made us, each and every one, He created a masterpiece, a one of a kind, with a will to live and a purpose to fulfil. Some of the great initiatives being implemented around the developing world are ingenious, innovative ideas created by and for the young people to sink their teeth into, to encourage and give them hope, not just a hand out, but something to give them dignity to invest their youth and energy into.

A little note to those reading who may be BEING led... remember to be an encourager to those who are leading you.

I cannot tell you how many times when I was IN the stretch, and someone from the team would write me a note, come alongside, bring around a meal, letting me know I was loved and appreciated. On some days it was the difference between wanting to run away, yet choosing to stand.

It's a fact that EVERYONE, whether young or old, rich or poor, black or white - we all need encouragement.

It's the fuel that sustains us, even in the hardest of times.

Job 4:4, 'Your words have upheld him who was stumbling, and you have strengthened the feeble knees.'

One of the most beautiful gifts in the world is the gift of encouragement. When someone encourages you, that person helps you over a threshold you might otherwise never have crossed on your own.4

John O'Donohue

the great generational transition

VALUE THREE: 20/20 DREAMS & VISIONS

HABAKKUK 2:2-3
AND THEN GOD ANSWERED: WRITE THIS.
WRITE WHAT YOU SEE. WRITE IT OUT IN BIG
BLOCK LETTERS SO THAT IT CAN BE READ
ON THE RUN. THIS VISION-MESSAGE IS A
WITNESS POINTING TO WHAT'S COMING. IT
ACHES FOR THE COMING—IT CAN HARDLY
WAIT! AND IT DOESN'T LIE. IF IT SEEMS SLOW
IN COMING, WAIT. IT'S ON ITS WAY. IT WILL
COME RIGHT ON TIME.

THE MESSAGE

I AM GRATEFUL to belong to a church that is always full of vision.

SO MUCH VISION...

Inspiring, breathtaking at times, and gives you more reasons every day to get up in the morning. Our Pastor, Brian Houston, says that we will always have way more vision than money... LOVE that.

The God gap is always there.

But seriously, I am completely honoured that I have grown up as part of a busy and genuine worship team, that during a mid-week rehearsal night, we are SO busy training and rehearsing and pouring over items and new songs, encouraging people, praying together, that by the time the night is over, we send people home exhausted and stretched, BUT made a little more aware of what they are truly capable of. And this is the fruit of seeing a vision inviting energy to our lives for a continued outworking of a greater vision.

It is true, without vision people perish, but with it, they SHINE.

I have spoken of this story often, that not long after I gave birth to our third daughter, Zoe Jewel, I was sitting with her in my arms at the kitchen table. It was a beautiful Sydney day, my other two girls were playing outside, and I just said to my husband with a contented sigh, 'I feel like I am living my dream', to which my husband quickly but lovingly replied, 'well, it's time to start dreaming bigger!'

I was at first shocked and unimpressed with his comments, but then I realised what he was saying.

If you stop dreaming, you get complacent, and complacency has never changed the world.

I guess for me to find energy and passion for what is in my heart, I have also been on the most valuable journey of growing in my understanding of the value of Calvary and all that Jesus has done for us. This makes me want to squeeze every drop out of opportunities we have to share Christ, to use our gifts and talents, however small or grandiose they may appear, and give Him the glory due His name, and to truly live a life that would be a life that worships the living God.

What this looks like for each one of us is different, but the goal of Acts 17 says that 'in Him we live and move and have our being'… that God Himself is there to be known by us, loved by us, all because He first loved us. But if we inadvertently preach a modern day Christianity of mediocrity, trying to water down what cost looks like or sharing a message of convenience, when we share Christ, it becomes more like presenting a lifestyle choice rather than the choice to lay down our lives and follow Him.

I said yes to Jesus, and said yes to ALL that that means, something to live and die for - a message of great grace, of great surrender, of forgiveness and healing, and of the greatest love you will ever know.

Out of the revelation of being loved, came VISION, which could only be explained as the eyes of my heart being opened and actually LOOKING for the promised HOPE.

The eyes of my heart found family, the church, and the encouragement and strength we have experienced over many years and many seasons has been superb, fuelling us in vigour and creativity!!

With vision came renewed passion, and with that passion I found energy for the adventure, and with that energy came a fresh confidence, a 'gift of confidence' I call it as I literally had very little before my Jesus-encounter.

So… for those of you lacking in sparkle for the future, whether you are young or old, in transition or not, it's time to start to dream about the things deep in your heart, to talk about the impossible coming to pass, and get the blinkers off the eyes of your heart… to get brave with VISION.

I have always LOVED this scripture about faith in Hebrews 11, 'Now faith is the substance of things hoped for, the evidence of things unseen'.

You see, FAITH - you cannot see it, but you can hang your life from it.

It's evident, but you cannot see it.

Vision has similar attributes, which is why in Habakkuk it says to write the vision down and make it plain, that those who see it may run with it.

Mark and I have endeavoured over the years to not just speak about what we see in our future, but write it down, read it, see where we are up to with it, and apart from this being of deep spiritual significance, it also keeps us accountable to staying on course. Where dreams and visions become extremely critical is when times are tough, when life has thrown you a curve ball, when the sun just doesn't seem to be shining as it should.

For then the written word becomes like a torch, reminding you of the possibilities that lie before you.

Many years ago I asked our team, 'what would you do with your life if there were no limits, no financial barriers, nothing in the way that you would consider to be holding you back?'

The answers were interesting and it became obvious to me that some of the team had given this a great deal of thought, but many had simply settled for very feasible outcomes. Many of the answers given I realised could quite easily be achieved with careful planning, some tenacity, and some good business sense. Actually, I felt quite burdened that night and ended up praying, 'God, how on earth do we encourage people to dream bigger, to think outside the box, to actually speak out and go for some of the desires in their hearts?'

For some people this actually comes quite easily, for others, this is more of a struggle. Lack of confidence, or a fear of what others will think can definitely inhibit your expression. Fear of comparison, fear of failing, all these REAL feelings can SO complicate your ability to communicate what is in your heart.

But as a leader today, and as one who is still discovering all that is in my heart, I encourage you to be brave and write down some of these unuttered passions. As Mother Teresa said, 'Yesterday is gone, tomorrow has not yet come, all we have is today. Let US BEGIN'.

It's hard to find your spiritual eyesight when you are weary, downcast, or even just tired. So sometimes, if you feel flat where vision is concerned, it may be as easy as getting some rest, tending to your soul, strengthening your inner man.

For me, I need to sit at my piano and just worship the Lord, open my Bible and simply sing. For some of you it may be as simple as getting outside in the fresh air, going for a walk, clearing your head, turning off the blackberry or phone, and just talk to God… to meditate and just embrace His Word working in your heart.

LOOK UP!!

One of the hardest things to find in our lives is time.

Time to listen, and to think, and to consider the stirrings in our hearts.

In seeing your future unfold, whether you are just starting out, starting again, or simply refining who it is you are becoming, there needs to be value placed on this kind of time. It may appear wasteful, but actually without seeing these times as important, your immediate concerns (which often scream louder than the less immediate), will take all of your time, with no planning or thought for future.

Billy Graham set a fine example and knew his life mission early which made his choices, his studies and his priorities all revolve around his inner resolve.

He said, 'My one purpose in life is to help people find a personal relationship with God, which I believe comes through knowing Christ'… His personal vision statement.

If you are concerned about getting it wrong, and missing the mark when it comes to God's best for you, take heart with this scripture.

Proverbs 16:9, 'in their hearts human beings plan their course, but the Lord establishes their steps'.

So I breathe a sigh of relief, and get going with what I have in my hand today, trusting the Lord to steer me in the right direction.

Another great reason to have your heart and mind filled with vision is that it keeps your mind from the past. Philippians 3:13 asks us to forget what is behind, and to reach toward all that is ahead. If all you have is a historical thought life, pressing forward is going to be difficult.

Many people's past is so real in them that it not only defines their future, but helps create it, for the Word says in Romans 23:7, 'that as a man thinks in his heart, so is he'. (AMP) Usually a hard past is entangled somehow in people disappointing us, and the key to a clean future is

FORGIVENESS.

You may have an incredible vision for your life, but if your heart is tangled in unfor-giveness, then all the vision in the world will not deal with that prickle. If you are a leader who is burdened and heavy with disillusionment, then you will carry this through to all in your sphere of influence until it is dealt with. So do whatever it is you need to do. Say sorry, seek some good counsel, go to your heavenly Father, and let's get healed and clean for all that lies ahead. And for those of you reading today who are just young in your journey of faith, and maybe your heart is filled with intense remorse or sadness, God is the answer every time. Go to Jesus with your concerns, again say you're sorry, put right what is wrong if it is in your power to do so, and move on.

And go back to writing down your dreams, your visions, your goals, your desires...

It is incredible to see those things that originally were simply a thought, a momen-tary, fleeting thought, actually come to life before your very eyes. I experience this often with songs. You know, I have ideas for songs, melodies, sounds, chords, lyrics all floating around in my heart and head (scary place to live at times!!), sometimes one foot in heaven, the other on earth, absolutely no use to anyone... aahhhhh.

That's how it is.

But hours or weeks or months later, I'll be singing that song to a congregation, or even more wild, they'll be singing it back to me, and I think about the power of bringing to the fore that which is in your heart. And it doesn't go from your heart to your hand by wishing it was there.

It comes by sticking at it, working, listening and learning, and living with that conviction that the Spirit of the Lord is upon my life for purpose.

Leaders… live dreaming!!

Dreamers who can communicate their heart are SO inspiring to be around.

Spend an afternoon with some of your team and ask them what they see for the future of the church! You will probably be pleasantly surprised at the depth of thought and passion you'll hear come from them.

DON'T be THREATENED!!

If your presence is a safe place for them to be in, you'll get to hear some of the most genuine and creative thoughts you've heard in a long time.

Recently I heard a young pastor stand for two minutes to share a thought on what he saw as the future of the church.

He humbly replied, 'I am not interested in being part of a contemporary church if it is not a church that is declaring the gospel… in our attempt to be relevant, let's not compromise what Jesus came and lived and died for.'

Amen to that.

What can you see for your life?

If all you see is NOT what you're believing for, then DON'T lose heart, for God's Word does not lie, and He is not a tease.

His ways are not our ways, He does not work by the world's standards or economies, and His heart is always for you.

So write it down, make it plain, dream big, go crazy!!

Who says you can't do all that is in your heart to do?

Inactivity is the thief of our times, but ACTIVITY with no purpose is also a thief, which again stresses the importance of VISION.

I would give all the wealth of the world, and all the deeds of all the heroes, for one true vision.5

Henry David Thoreau

the great generational transition

VALUE FOUR: ENERGY

PHILIPPIANS 2:12

WHAT I'M GETTING AT, FRIENDS, IS THAT YOU
SHOULD SIMPLY KEEP ON DOING WHAT YOU'VE DONE
FROM THE BEGINNING. WHEN I WAS LIVING AMONG
YOU, YOU LIVED IN RESPONSIVE OBEDIENCE. NOW
THAT I'M SEPARATED FROM YOU, KEEP IT UP. BETTER
YET, REDOUBLE YOUR EFFORTS. BE ENERGETIC IN
YOUR LIFE OF SALVATION, REVERENT AND SENSITIVE
BEFORE GOD. THAT ENERGY IS GOD'S ENERGY, AN
ENERGY DEEP WITHIN YOU, GOD HIMSELF WILLING
AND WORKING AT WHAT WILL GIVE HIM THE MOST
PLEASURE.

THE MESSAGE

I GUESS it is unusual to call energy a value, and yet, without it, most of what I am outlining in this book is hard to achieve. AND yet it is one of those indefinables that people are always searching for more of but can't quite get there on their own. In most doctors' surgeries, you'll find one of the most popular complaints is that people have no energy, and often are going through the motions of activity without connection, leaving them internally quite depressed.

These are very real feelings, and can be quite catatonic for the one experiencing them.

But John 10:10 talks about us having life, and life in all its fullness.

That sounds like energy to me!!

In leadership, if you are trying to bring any sense of NEW to the table as far as your life goes, energy is one of the essential ingredients.

You can feed your energy levels or starve them, depending on what you hear, what you read, the conversation you engage in, the company you keep, the thoughts you dwell on.

Yes, everything can affect your energy levels, and I have found that when leading others,

GREAT energy is expended AND expected.

The story of the Israelite people who were SO in the wilderness, who had to go every single morning and gather up fresh manna, food from heaven to sustain them on a daily basis, reveals a God principle for all of us. For we need to be fuelled, inspired from God Himself with His answers and supply for every day.

We do this by reading the Word of God, I mean really reading it, and welcoming the power of the Word in our lives.

We are fuelled as we worship Him, lifting our voices, bringing our prayers and thanksgiving and truly and simply worshipping, just singing our love song to Him.

And we are ultimately fuelled and fulfilled in serving Him.

My husband Mark is a great collector of old and rare books written to keep a record of the lives of great men and woman who've gone before. These books are filled with miracle stories of the unrelenting faithfulness of God, recounting times of incredible revival and again and again tell stories of how God moved into a village and brought salvation AND social reform. I cannot get enough of these books into me… the stories are crazy, and the inspiration endless! There are also often inscriptions at the front of these books with handwritten encouragements from one disciple to another on their journey of faith.

One book entitled 'Men of Fire', written by Walter Russell Bowie (1961), says right at the top 'to the men of Virginia seminary who for many generations have carried the gospel fire'.

This line alone intrigued me and caused me to spend time researching this man's life, and find out about his salvation experience, to learn about his passion for Christ, to learn about the fire of God in him that caused him to live a life that made a difference.

I found a man who had energy for relationships, study, marriage, and was involved in taking the gospel to as many as he could throughout his life. His biography reads that he was a priest, author, educator, hymn writer, and lecturer in the Episcopal Church.

Bowie was ordained as a priest in 1909, serving at three Episcopalian churches and two theological seminaries. He served as a Red Cross chaplain at Base Hospital 45 in France during World War I. And he was greatly known for standing up for the impoverished and making a difference… the Social Gospel gaining great momentum through his life of faith AND works. And he talks of the fire of conviction, the fire of the Holy Spirit, this unrelenting LIFE force at work in him, producing an energy that could not be explained away.

I love that he penned a book that would stir his own spirit and the spirit of many others like myself, with so many stories of men who had a conversion experience that could not be denied, and one of the great by-products of this new life experience was energy for the journey. Over and over the story is told - that when you have not only vision and focus but Holy Spirit fire alive in you, energy comes. Isaiah 40:31, 'but those who hope in the LORD will renew their strength. They will soar on wings like eagles; they will run and not grow weary, they will walk and not be faint.'

Once we had the privilege of holding a worship conference in Toulon, France, and were hosted by an incredible group of nuns, who were generous to the core, their service humbling us in a way that I pray will always impact my life. Many of the people present on the day were so enthusiastic in their faith, and wanted to keep talking to us about the FIRE in their belly for the things of God. There was such hunger for more of only what God had in store, just devoted Christ followers who were giving up their jobs and living by faith to travel wherever they could to share their faith and hope in God. I heard the word 'salvation' so many times, as young men and women just poured out the contents of their hearts to myself and the team, aching for God to move in their city.

Wow, I just want to get up and declare over nations Chris Tomlin's song 'God of this City'6 - Bring it on!

Of course, this fire I keep referring to is what people for generations have come to use as a term to describe the Holy Spirit, and in reading of the saints of old, to hearing life stories from the saints of today, and from our own personal experience, there is a power available to us through the third person of the Trinity, the Holy Spirit, that cannot be explained away, however hard some may try.

In Acts 1:8 the Word says that 'You will receive power when the Holy Spirit comes upon you, and you will be His witnesses to the ends of the earth.' Again, the energy and life available to us is very real and very attainable to see His will done on the earth.

Romans 15:13 says, 'may the God of hope fill you with all joy and peace as you trust in Him, so that you may overflow with hope, by the power of the Holy Spirit.'

Such great news - not by might or by power, but by the Spirit of God.
This means that you don't have to have a sanguine personality to lead or follow

with energy, but bringing the energy that HOPE creates by the Spirit of God.

I always find it inspiring to watch many of the great achievers in life bring their energy and focus to their particular passion, as when the energy is flowing from a healthy place, and the desired outcomes are clear, the disciplines required to achieve the outcome come a little easier when your goal is in your constant view, either in your heart, or in the natural.

And when the bedrock of all you are living for is Christ and His Kingdom, there is no life sustaining force like it.

One of my dear friends who had been dealing with some depression in her life had been finding she had no energy for anything, which was really out of character for her. I asked her a few questions as all her kids were growing up and leaving home. Life will never be as it was with little ones running about your feet and you as their superstar.

Tough to let go.

Anyway, I asked her what would she be doing if she could do anything she wanted; what was it she loved to do and what was her key passion or gift? She went very quiet and ended up crying and crying as she realised she'd forgotten what made her come alive as far as contributing to church or society, and that now that her kids don't need her EVERY day, well depression was just waiting with his nasty claws just around the corner to have his way. But my friend is a champion, and finally after having a revelation one day that she would never encounter great energy again while she remained so down in herself, she is SO on her way back to a sense of a new horizon over her future.

Now THAT is energising.

Years ago at one of our church staff meetings, Pastor Jonathan Wilson, who now pastors a great church in California, spoke about energy, and said,

"If you want to reap energy, you have to sow energy."

Simple yet profound.

I found that once I turned forty, I seriously had to up my exercise routine, and start running, to keep my natural energy levels up.

We reap what we sow.

Likewise, the older I get and the more church services and meetings I am a part of, ALL the more do I need to be found in His Word, embracing God's pattern and teaching for myself, not just hearing more messages, but digging into the WORD myself... hungry for His presence to be evident and outworked through my life.

If you wonder how on earth you are going to find it in yourself to LIFT again, to bring an energy that you feel isn't even there for this next season, then it's time to start sowing energy!!

Much of life is quite routine as far as living each day goes. Waking up, getting dressed and fed, dressing and feeding and prepping all the others in your home for the day, making beds, laundry, meetings, cooking, shopping, teaching, homework, rehearsals... aaahh, the glamour life!!

But when you walk out your days with Godly intent, there is definitely a renewed energy found.

I believe as a leader, that we must display consistencies in our approach of leadership and in our lifestyle habits that are tried and true and are non-negotiable, and leaning into Holy Spirit infused energy is one of them. It's very frustrating to be around leaders who are SO filled with energy for an idea, then we all get behind it, then the idea wanes, so does the energy, and we end up starting the cycle again. Up and down is the cycle, rather than strength to strength, and these kinds of behaviours will certainly damage the health of the team.

Energetic, God-loving people serving leadership creates such a faith-filled culture that we are left with no room for the silliness, the bickering, the normal stuff you get when there is a bunch of us working together and doing life together.

An energetic culture is created through consistency, a culture of everyone partici-pating, a culture of life and hope, a culture of great faith and expectancy, a culture where wins are celebrated, and a culture where God-encounter bringing change in our lives is the constant expectation.

Now, it's certainly not time to get into a works-based theology and wear yourself out by trying to become some kind of super human, but let's peel back the layers and see what could build energy into YOU and your team.

CLARITY.

It's easy for people to follow with enthusiasm when they know where you're go-ing. Our Pastor has made it so clear for the church by stating his vision statement whenever he can, and over years and years, this keeps clarity and builds trust. We know where we're going, the goal hasn't changed, and so we RUN with that goal in mind and there is energy for the ride.

For the worship team there is, to the best of our ability, a clear way forward to become involved in the team, a clear way forward to become part of the fabric of that team, and a high but realistic expectation from us all to bring our best. Clear objectives, unhindered energy.

GOOD FOOD.

Now I am not going to go into a spiel about health and fitness although I could. But I will just throw in here that whenever there are especially busy seasons ap-proaching, we are always saying to the team to get plenty of rest and eat well and exercise, so as boring and practical as that is, it is also CRITCAL to longevity and increased energy levels rather than a perpetual state of tiredness. I've learned never to presume that people know how to take care of themselves. In this very parentless generation, the practical simple things are often not taught.

What I actually mean about GOOD FOOD, is to make sure you are all receiving good solid Biblical teaching every chance you get.

You can try and pump yourself up without it for a day, a week, a month or two even… but sustainability in energy in the end needs to be fuelled from the inside out through the LIVING Word of God.

That's one of the reasons we need to continually meet together as a church body, to receive the Word of God and be fuelled for life.

JOY.

Finding your joy is one thing, keeping it is another.

But true joy is not circumstance-dependent; it is a fruit of the Spirit, and one that I treasure in my life.

Isaiah 60:1 says, 'Arise and shine for your light has come. Nations will come to your light'.

Verse 5 says, 'you will look and be radiant'.

Verse 15 says, 'I will make you the everlasting pride and the joy of all generations!'

Lead the team with joy, lead your home with joy, lead yourself with joy!!

Joy brings LIFE!! You know in our team, when I would walk in full of joy, it brought SECURITY to the atmosphere. No drama queens allowed!! Joy unspeakable and full of glory.

No joy, no songs, no energy for praise, no energy for life.

When Job was at his all time lowest, his anguished soul cried out and said there was no longer a shout of joy heard from his land.

When my own soul was down about how I would ever lead a team of worshippers, the Lord took me to Psalm 45:7 where it says,

'You love righteousness and hate wickedness; therefore God, your God, has set you above your companions by anointing you with the oil of joy.'

I was SO relieved. Even though I knew so little about leadership, I knew I could lead with joy, by grace.

CREATIVITY

OK, getting creative might take a bit of energy, but our creative nature is essential to who we are as human beings, as being made in the image of Christ.

Such joy springs out from the heart of one who has created something out of nothing, or order out of chaos.

Fruitfulness is what we are created for. So sometimes, just to stir up your energy levels, all you may need to do is something creative!

As children of the Author of creation itself, of the One who flung the stars into space, who paints majestic sunsets every night only to paint a new one tomorrow, who intricately and lovingly handcrafted each one of us for His pleasure... we should not be surprised therefore at our need to create.

And for some of you who started out in a creative expression in your leadership role who have ended up becoming facilitators of rosters and schedules, line-ups and arrangements... mmm, I think I've found your answer to gather some energy for the road. Be inspired, you'll find yourself SO much more inspiring!

SO, hear my heart as I say... to bring energy to the leadership table you need to firstly take a breath and rest in God's grace, and welcome the Holy Spirit into the situation, listening to God speaking to your heart for your particular circumstance. Then once you have direction, keep delighting yourself in the Lord and watch Him bring your heart's desire to pass... and serve Him with gladness.

You can do it.

Joy motivates, sadness is heavy.

Be brave in your pursuit of HIS LIFE IN YOUR VEINS.

2 Timothy 2:1-7, 'So, my son, throw yourself into this work for Christ. Pass on what you heard from me—the whole congregation saying Amen!— to reliable leaders who are competent to teach others. When the going gets rough, take it on the chin with the rest of us, the way Jesus did. A soldier on duty doesn't get caught up in making deals at the marketplace. He concentrates on carrying out orders. An athlete who refuses to play by the rules will never get anywhere. It's the diligent farmer who gets the produce. Think it over. God will make it all plain'.
(The Message)

You only lose energy when life becomes dull in your mind. Your mind gets bored and therefore tired of doing nothing. Get interested in something! Get absolutely enthralled in something! Get out of yourself! Be somebody! Do something. The more you lose yourself in something bigger than yourself, the more energy you will have.7

Norman Vincent Peale

the great generational transition

VALUE FIVE: THE SQUEEZE

JAMES 1:2
CONSIDER IT A SHEER GIFT, FRIENDS, WHEN TESTS
AND CHALLENGES COME AT YOU FROM ALL SIDES.
YOU KNOW THAT UNDER PRESSURE, YOUR FAITH-
LIFE IS FORCED INTO THE OPEN AND SHOWS ITS
TRUE COLOURS. SO DON'T TRY TO GET OUT OF
ANYTHING PREMATURELY. LET IT DO ITS WORK SO
YOU BECOME MATURE AND WELL-DEVELOPED, NOT
DEFICIENT IN ANY WAY.

THE MESSAGE

'CONSIDER IT PURE JOY', says James. OK, not my first thought when the squeeze is on, but OK joy, here we come!

Hard work, pressure - the squeeze creating endurance - fantastic! But how much pressure is too much pressure? I think of this in the context of raising champion teams, of growing strength in people, of inspiring more people than ever to go the extra mile in serving Christ.

I have been asked the question SO many times on how much is too much and it has certainly given me much to ponder over of late.

The reason for including this as a value, is that I know beyond a shadow of a doubt, that when the pressure is on and you feel you may almost break, there is GREAT GROWTH going on, on the inside, and yet our natural tendency is to mini-mise discomforts from our lives if we can. But without the stretch, you will never know what you are capable of.

Even on a musical level, we have had to work very hard to now have a level of playing that is consistently strong. It has not come by just crossing our fingers and hoping everyone has listened to the CD at home to practice to. It has come over consistent rehearsals - late if need be - over years and years, to ensure we are bringing our best. Our best has definitely got better, but it hasn't come through wishing. And what has emerged though, it wasn't part of the plan, was that I found that hard work on any gift means the ordinary has a chance to become extraordinary.

A culture of hard work never hurt anyone, as long as you have the goal in sight. And to me, that is the strength of the church; everyone can come and be included in the great manifesto of praise that has silenced the enemy from the beginning of time.

Just on that, if you don't rehearse, and become reliant on the very gifted who may have no need to rehearse, then you will eventually shrink your team UP... so you end up with the naturally gifted being able to contribute, but without a 'replacing yourself' model which constantly is in a training process with as many as you can handle. One day you may just stand still and wonder where everyone has gone.

I sat in a leadership meeting one day talking over changes that were being made for our church family on weekends. The changes were SO, SO good, asking the church to come to one service on the weekend, and then serve in one service on the weekend - receiving and serving.

Stunning for the church, and stunning to keep the culture of servanthood right in the middle of our DNA.

But I must have started thinking as I became very quiet, and I was asked 'why the contemplative mood?' I started to share with the other leaders, that although I knew this was the way forward for us and such a strong way forward, I asked the question... would we still have access to 'the squeeze'? For what I know with my own life and the life of many that I literally do life with, is that without some of that pressure we've experienced over the years, then I just don't know that we'd be doing what we're doing. The stretch has given ordinary people like myself a chance to see what we're really capable of. And my greatest fear would be that those coming behind would never have to experience the absolute knowledge that if this isn't God, if He doesn't shine here, we're toast!!

This area of thought is, for me personally, one of the great faith adventures that I feel has been paramount to where the church finds herself today.

We live in a world of short cuts and quick fixes, the lotto generation, waiting for a wad of cash to come falling from the sky. Yet in life, all of the greatest things take time, and energy, and care, developing patience through the waiting.

Delayed gratification is one the hardest things this generation deals with, as if they can't have it now, or at least soon, let's try something else.

Churches all over the world have said no to convenience, to make sure their churches are found in the middle of villages, cities and the like; and have found themselves prepping school halls and community centres from 4am in the morning, putting chairs out and little PA systems to make church great.

And it's not anything new.

For generations, men and women of God have worked hard and defied all odds to bring the gospel to all men. And this is what I'm talking about - these times of stretching ourselves, being generous with our time and resource, working together to see the church be all she can be... simply stunning.

But to deprive our children and our spiritual children of these building blocks in life means we are short changing them when it comes to building tenacity and spiritual muscle. Even though we do not want to create silly hardships for them so that we can prove a point, there needs to come a time when they feel the weight of responsibility on their shoulders.

Whenever any of us are confronted with a test - a relational issue, a patience issue, a finance issue, a submission issue, whatever it may be - we need to remember that tests help define what we truly believe, and continue to help craft who we are. I have had so many stretching times, as we all have, and I have had to learn to yield when I don't understand, and be quiet when I feel like saying my piece, but the scriptures instruct me to know my place and know the heart of my God toward us all, and that He is in control.

And how we handle the stretch is the most important thing of all.

Are you very bendable? Very flexible? Are you willing to listen or do you have an opinion set in stone? Good questions to ask yourself, as remaining flexible is also a good key to remember while remaining sane through change!

One of the young guys at church, Jonathon Douglass (or JD), has been part of our church for his whole life. And I have watched him grow and shine, and I have seen him transition from follower to leader with great dignity and strength of character. It has been a journey, but seriously, his parents have never allowed their children to shortcut through any of the journey, even though their kids are well known and well loved and could probably slip through without any obvious immediate conse-quences. No, their kids have learned to carry the load, to follow through, to stay and pack up, to not quit, to lead people by loving them and believing in them.

These are the lessons that true champions learn.

If you watch any champion team in training, they don't just 'have a go' and hope they'll make it to the top. No, they push themselves to the limit, push their bodies and see what they are capable of.

And does it hurt? YES and YES and YES again!

Would they be key players in a key team without it? NO and NO and NO.

I heard Sy Rogers speak recently of the seasons in life historically and how these seasons have also affected the way we parent our children and subsequently, lead others; generations who have pushed their kids way too hard and shown no mercy or emotion on the way, raising stoic 'get the job done', 'don't hug me' children, and 'never be seen crying' men. Right to the other extreme of molly-coddling our babies, wrapping them in cotton wool, trying to protect them from any measure of pain that may edge up alongside them in life.

Neither is ideal, but the story inside the story, is that while trying to protect our kids from everything, we strengthen them for nothing, raise them to hide, and train them to run from conflict. The meeting in the middle is that to train them to lead, they have to partake in all that life has to offer, the highs and the lows, yet be given the tools to overcome the trials, and share in the seasons of blessing.

So, in endeavouring to raise a strong team and not a team of spiritual babies, the teaching that came to my heart was simply this,

that in the stretch, you've got to learn to STAND.

THE FULFILMENT OF MINISTRY, THE REASON YOU WERE PUT ON THIS EARTH, IS A DIRECT RESULT OF YOUR RELATIONSHIP WITH CHRIST. KNOWING GOD, AND BEARING FRUIT.

THE MESSAGE OF JOHN 15.

BUT THE CRITICAL ELEMENT, LEARNING HOW TO STAND, TO REMAIN SECURE AT YOUR POST IS ONE OF THE MOST POWERFUL PIECES OF KNOWLEDGE YOU CAN ATTAIN.

Standing while being stretched is not easy; we want to run and hide, run and take the pressure off. But rather than running, I love the thought of His presence over-shadowing me AS I stand.

Covered by His mighty wing.

In times of the squeeze, bring to mind that YOU WERE DESIGNED FOR A MIS-SION.

Acts 20:24, 'the most important thing is that I complete my mission, the work that the Lord Jesus Christ gave me.' Our English word, mission, comes from the Latin word for 'sending'.

We have been sent on a mission.

To be part of writing an incredible history to be inspirational for others; to be part of breaking ground so that others can partake of an incredible future; and to live purposefully in the moment that is entrusted to us right now. I love that thought of generational consistency and that if we live with strength, imagine what the next generation will do.

We continue Jesus' mission on earth as we 'go to all the people of all the nations and make them disciples.' (Matthew 28:19)

When you understand that what you are involved with on earth - whether it is being part of a team, at home raising a family, working, or at school - when you see it as MISSION rather than a task, you will have a greater resolve to STAND.

COUNT THE COST

ABANDONING agenda, laying down your life is costly, but oh so wonderful. Jesus prayed, 'Father, not my will but Yours be done'. You stop praying self-focused prayers like, "God, bless what I want to do". The Bible says, give yourself com-pletely to God – every part – to be tools in His hand, to be used for His good purposes.

No longer I that lives, but Christ who lives in me.

DECIDE NOW, WHEN IT GETS TOO HARD, THAT YOU'VE ALREADY DECIDED TO PAY WHATEVER THE COST.

Imagine if every woman who has ever given birth decided just before the baby was born to say, OK, I'm not doing this. Too hard. It's all over (actually, I'm sure I said that right before delivery). But even though birth is painful (massive understatement) the result is so great there are not enough words to explain.

When I am running (and I use the word running loosely!!) and it gets hard, everything in me wants to give up, but because I want to improve, I push my body to go a little further every time, to build my strength and stamina. Not easy, but I must run that little bit further every time to make sure I am improving.

Likewise, in the seasons of shift and change and challenge, you learn to STRENGTHEN YOUR SPIRITUAL MUSCLE.

EVERY time you are faced with a choice of standing or drooping, staying or leaving, getting up or staying in bed... flex your muscles, MUSCLES NEED TO BE STRENGTHENED and the only way this will happen is by USE.

One great road to strength is called PRAYER.

Oswald Chambers says, 'Prayer is the vital breath of the Christian, not the thing that makes him alive, but the evidence that He is alive!!!'

One day while overhearing someone outside my office complaining about how much work he had to do as a volunteer, I went to walk out to console him and maybe take the workload down a bit for him. But as soon as I got up I felt the Lord speak to me in my spirit saying, 'NO, I am doing a work in him.' So, I went out and just thanked him for all he does and said how much we appreciate him, and then went back to my office. In the end, all I can do as a leader, is to ask God for wisdom to make great decisions and for grace when I make incorrect ones, and to realise that in the end, people are in God's hands, and they make their own decisions and need to walk out the consequences of those decisions.

So, as a leader, teach people how to stand, how to enjoy hard work for a greater purpose, and above all, how to PRAY. It's not our job to simply tell people what to do, it's our job to lead them to the Father so that they can hear what He wants them to do.

MMMM, the squeeze..... Bring it on.

When we long for life without difficulties, remind us that oaks grow strong in contrary winds and diamonds are made under pressure.[8]

Peter Marshall

the great generational transition

VALUE SIX: OPEN DOORS

TITUS 2:1
YOUR JOB IS TO SPEAK OUT ON THE THINGS THAT
MAKE FOR SOLID DOCTRINE. GUIDE OLDER MEN
INTO LIVES OF TEMPERANCE, DIGNITY, AND WISDOM,
INTO HEALTHY FAITH, LOVE, AND ENDURANCE. GUIDE
OLDER WOMEN INTO LIVES OF REVERENCE SO THEY
END UP AS NEITHER GOSSIPS NOR DRUNKS, BUT
MODELS OF GOODNESS. BY LOOKING AT THEM, THE
YOUNGER WOMEN WILL KNOW HOW TO LOVE THEIR
HUSBANDS AND CHILDREN, BE VIRTUOUS AND PURE,
KEEP A GOOD HOUSE, BE GOOD WIVES. WE DON'T
WANT ANYONE LOOKING DOWN ON GOD'S MESSAGE
BECAUSE OF THEIR BEHAVIOUR. ALSO, GUIDE THE
YOUNG MEN TO LIVE DISCIPLINED LIVES.

THE MESSAGE

APART FROM WHEN I'm writing, I like to have my door open. Whether it's at an office or at home, I like that open feeling, so that friends feel welcome to just come on in. When I was working in our church offices, I also loved to have my door open, apart from the first few weeks of a new college term when overseas students would walk past slowly to get a good look in! Sometimes I felt like I should charge a fee and raise some dollars for missions!

As funny as that sounds, I became increasingly aware of the fact that for many of the guys and gals coming through, many who are without strong role models in the natural, are looking for far more than understanding how to lead worship, but they want to know how to live life. I discovered this many years ago at one of our conferences, when I opened up the floor for questions.

There were a couple of nicely packaged questions regarding musical transitions in worship, and myself and others answered to the best of our ability. But then, after an uncomfortable silence, one of the delegates said, "Can I ask something of a more personal nature?"

"Sure", I replied, wondering where this would go. But seriously, if you have nothing to hide, you shouldn't feel nervous.

Well, this guy started asking about the tension he was feeling between expectation from leadership, versus expectation from home, and the conversation that followed was Godly and not at all aggressive, AND it opened up a huge amount of questions that people don't know who to ask or how to ask. We answered him by saying that he had to take responsibility for home by NOT playing church off against his family, and that healthy conversations needed to be had to put things right.

As leaders we should always consider the outfall of what we ask people to do BEFORE we ask it as, because people are so kind hearted, they will often say yes to honour us, and home takes a back seat again. I am all for throwing people in the deep end, getting them to serve HARD, but not at the expense of others.

The questions continue thick and fast to this day. They want to know how to get married and stay married. They want to know how to stay on fire for the things of God and how to not get weary. They want to know how to run their finances, they want to know how to run a home, how to cook, they want to know when the right time is to have children, and they want to know now! They want to know what the Bible says about homosexuality, about divorce, about tithing, about the Kingdom of God; they want to know how to handle success, and how to handle disappointments.

And so the 'open door' philosophy was born. Our lives were available to be read, to be followed, to be questioned. And I started to arm myself with Biblical answers for everyday situations. AND, I learned quickly that I didn't have to be the expert, I just had to do what I could, always pray with people, and point them to Christ and make sure I had enough margin in my day to be more available. When needed. On purpose.

In the end it's all about loving the people, being a good shepherd, and being aware of other things that may be going on in their private world so you can be a support.

Being available for the team was probably the greatest challenge for Mark and I personally, not just because there are only so many hours in a day, but because over the years I've become quite precious of my time with family. But being available is such a gift to someone who is looking for a mentor leader, just needing someone to show them the way.

One of the great ways to connect with people is just to learn to linger. Don't always be the first one to leave, but look forward to hanging around a little while after a service, actually PLAN to stay back after a rehearsal, whatever it may be, and LISTEN to what people are saying. Don't look past them to check out what's going on in the background.

CONNECT!

With the open door theory, I love to have people in my home, chatting to them while we are just doing life. Rather than having meetings and more meetings, invite someone to your home to chat while you potter at home, bring them over to be with you while you write a song, if you are driving the kids around, going to the airport, make a point to grab one of the young ones who's been asking to have time with you and just get them involved in the real world.

You see, without an open door policy, for those we influence we foster an imaginary notion of what life in ministry looks like. There have been so many times in my life when I have been buying groceries or dropping off the dry cleaning, picking up the kids from school, and people literally stop me to ask me if this is REALLY what I do when I am not on a platform. Scary stuff! But in this culture of celebrity, there is a world created in the minds of many people that is almost more real to them than their real world existence, and unfortunately, with so much of the world's mentality seeping into the church unchallenged, a sub-culture within a church culture creates itself as the goal to pursue.

We do live within a culture that urges us to take control of our own lives, to become equipped to be masters of our own destinies, to do whatever we need to do to get to the top, and then somehow use the Bible to support our notions. But that is not the way the Word of God was given to infuse us. The Bible was not written as a handy script to adapt or modify, to fit into our particular situation.

Eugene Peterson said it like this, 'The author of THE book is writing us into His book, we aren't writing Him into ours. We find ourselves in the book as followers of Jesus. Jesus calls us to follow Him and obey or we do not.'[9]

SO we raise, and train and love people TO the Lord, not our own version of what this is.

So leaders, I put the challenge out to you! IS your life a door open or door closed life? Do you put out a vibe that you welcome questions or are you a 'don't go there' type of leader?

It's that whole area of our UNSEEN lives - our Monday to Saturday - to use a phrase by Pastor Bill Hybels, it's 'who you are when no-one's looking'.

Some of the super practical areas that we can easily address are things like teaching the team what healthy boundaries are in life and how to put them into place. Because everything we do is a seed sown, the importance of making healthy choices is supreme, and when there are just NO boundaries, lives quickly get out of balance. Do a teaching series on what BALANCE looks like day to day.

How do we achieve balance?

Answer their questions through the Word of God.

TEACH them.

And whatever you are not sure of, learn it, then go teach it!

I recently had to write down a morning routine for someone in my world who just wasn't coping with getting on with the day. Too basic you think? Doesn't relate to how you lead? Think again lovely one, for when the basics in life are sloppy, so will other areas of your life follow suit. How to develop discipline for each day is an extremely important principle to teach our children, natural or spiritual... reading the Word, developing your gift, in being a punctual responsible human being, becoming more generous, the list is endless.

Even more practically, (I know you men are now reeling) things like how to dress, what is acceptable and what is not. Many young women today are being raised by the fashion industry rather than mentors or family, and it only takes a little bit of time and a little bit of care to teach the young what is right. It's not about style or flair, all of that stuff is fine and fun. No, it's about Holiness, that's our standard. Treating our body as a temple of the Holy Spirit and teaching our kids to honour that.

And leaders, PLEASE don't sit in judgement of young men or women that don't dress or look like what you'd prefer. Spiritual transformation takes place on the inside and then over time works its way through the whole of our beings. I get very upset when young people are discounted because of how they look, or how things 'appear' to be. God views us from a whole different perspective. He formed us, cell by cell, wove within our framework a need for Him and a need to accomplish purpose.

John 4:35, 'Do you not say, "Four months more and then the harvest"? I tell you, open your eyes and look at the fields! They are ripe for harvest.'

We are told to OPEN our eyes, the harvest is there and ready. But you know, the harvest doesn't look like it used to. It is covered in tattoos and needle-marks, and scars from slashed wrists and earrings in every possible place, but we love the harvest. And more importantly, God so loved us, every one of us, that He gave His finest to bring redemption for us.

Now that's the finest example there is.

Do all the good you can, by all the means you can, in all the ways you can, in all the places you can, at all the times you can, to all the people you can, as long as ever you can.[10]

John Wesley

the great generational transition

VALUE SEVEN: EXCELLENCE

2 CHRONICLES 2:5
THE HOUSE I AM BUILDING HAS TO BE THE BEST,
FOR OUR GOD IS THE BEST, FAR BETTER THAN
COMPETING GODS. BUT WHO IS CAPABLE OF
BUILDING SUCH A STRUCTURE?
WHY, THE SKIES—THE ENTIRE COSMOS!—CAN'T
BEGIN TO CONTAIN HIM. AND ME, WHO AM I TO
THINK I CAN BUILD A HOUSE ADEQUATE FOR
GOD—BURNING INCENSE TO HIM IS ABOUT ALL
I'M GOOD FOR! I NEED YOUR HELP: SEND ME A
MASTER ARTISAN IN GOLD, SILVER, BRONZE, IRON,
TEXTILES OF PURPLE, CRIMSON, AND VIOLET, AND
WHO KNOWS THE CRAFT OF ENGRAVING; HE WILL
SUPERVISE THE TRAINED CRAFTSMEN IN JUDAH
AND JERUSALEM THAT MY FATHER PROVIDED.
ALSO SEND CEDAR, CYPRESS, AND ALGUM LOGS
FROM LEBANON; I KNOW YOU HAVE LUMBERJACKS
EXPERIENCED IN THE LEBANON FORESTS.
I'LL SEND WORKERS TO JOIN YOUR CREWS TO CUT
PLENTY OF TIMBER—I'M GOING TO NEED A LOT,
FOR THIS HOUSE I'M BUILDING IS GOING TO BE
ABSOLUTELY STUNNING—
A SHOWCASE TEMPLE!' .

THE MESSAGE

RECENTLY I WAS ASKED the question, 'What makes someone a Worship Pastor?' I took a moment while it felt like a thousand thoughts went through my mind. Skill sets, musical ability, anointing, calling, yes I knew that all the answers I could give would be correct in some form or another, but the words that eventually came were simple.

'You have to care', was my reply. And the reason WHY you care is very important. You have to care enough to protect the truth of the unfolding revelation of God in our midst. You have to care about the people you have been entrusted with to shepherd, more than many of the other urgent requests that come through your inbox. You have to care about the theology being taught through the singing of songs, and care that we bring these anthems of praise to the best of our ability.

The fact is, the only way that you will bring authenticity and excellence to anything you are putting your hand to is because you care. And care comes in response to us valuing certain things in our lives, that we will do anything to care for them appropriately.

'For God so loved... that He gave.' God's giving was not out of obligation, but was motivated by love, which demanded a response of excellence.

I believe that any form of honest leadership requires the leader to teach the young the most EXCELLENT way. Not the easy way or a shortcut way for a quick fix compromise. This will never provide a strong enough foundation for the future to lean on.

EXCELLENCE is a standard we cannot afford to stray from.

The intro scripture of this chapter finds the words of a man impassioned to only bring the finest he can possibly lay his hands on for the temple of God. Not excellence to please the eyes of man, excellence fuelled from a heart that cared that God's house was given the finest attention possible.

I mention this next particular scripture a lot because I believe it is so significant when it comes to the word 'excellence'.

2 Samuel 24, from verse 20...

20-21 'Araunah looked up and saw David and his men coming his way; he met them, bowing deeply, honouring the king and saying, "Why has my master the king come to see me?"

"To buy your threshing floor," said David, "so I can build an altar to God here and put an end to this disaster."

22-23 "Oh," said Araunah, "let my master the king take and sacrifice whatever he wants. Look, here's an ox for the burnt offering and threshing paddles and ox-yokes for fuel—Araunah gives it all to the king! And may God, your God, act in your favour."

24-25 But the king said to Araunah, "No. I've got to buy it from you for a good price; I'm not going to offer God, my God, sacrifices that are no sacrifice."'
(The Message)

David was certainly in a season of his life where God was dealing with his disobedience, and David certainly didn't have a lot to bargain with when it came to God and him. But these scriptures do reveal David's heart again as he was not willing to compromise the truth of his sacrifice to the Lord to appease the eyes of man. And this, my friend, describes a commitment again to excellence that is fuelled by a desire to please God. Beautiful!!

I know that excellence is such a showy word and it does turn a lot of people off. The Message Bible actually uses the word BEST to describe excellence in a more earthy tone.

To bring excellence in your craft takes a lot of time and dedication. To bring excellence in your home takes all you have and more for your family to continually have access to your best. To serve with excellence in our local church and community will require you to be more thoughtful and tenacious than you possibly ever felt you could be. And we go the extra mile because we care. Yes, excellence takes more time, more heart, and more devotion than you thought you had in you.

I care so much that worship being offered from the house of God anywhere would be the purest we have for that moment. Not showy or 'spectacular' but earnest and thoughtful. And I desire to always live in that revelation.

The opposite of what this ideally looks like is careless worship. And by that I mean exactly how it reads. LESS CARE. Worship that may even sound and look good, but when it comes to the real truth of the goals here, there is little or no care. Teaching this kind of excellence is not that hard, but it will be seen through consistency of what is acceptable and what is not. So, like most of the other values, the WHY behind the WHAT of truth takes time. Again, as leaders, investing your time and your testimony and your stories about lessons you have learned in this regard are invaluable. Teach your wisdom, and invest your energies into those who you can... otherwise excellence becomes reduced to rules and boundaries that make no sense.

Teach the WHY behind all you do.

No one said raising children was ever easy.

Mel and Matt Hope, some of our closest friends and one couple we do a lot of life with, a few years ago picked up their young family and spent some time in Rwanda, East Africa, as part of the Hope Rwanda project team. Matt oversees the building of the homes in the Hope Village, and so they took a whole bunch of builders and labourers to help get some momentum going on the ground. We wanted to make sure the buildings were of a specific quality to ensure they would be standing well into the future.

The skilled builders spent so much of their time and effort training up the unskilled locals who, in the past, had built a lot of homes out of necessity, and even though they were of an ingenious design, these homes were not built to last. The task to teach was long and sometimes painful... one wall had to be erected and then pulled down and re-erected four times until the process was correct, but stability was the result, and CARE was the driver.

Don't make the lessons too easy... all the best things in life take

CARE + TIME + ENERGY.

In Genesis 4, the age old story of Cain and Abel, where we are told that the Lord accepted Abel's offering, his 'choice' offering, but Cain's offering, not his finest, the Lord did not accept. The Lord speaks to Cain and says 'that if you do not do what is right, sin is waiting at your door, for it desires to have you, but you must master it.' (verse 7)

Excellence in bringing our lives as an offering is something we continually ask the Holy Spirit to teach us about, so that we may master the art of bringing our best always, and that it may be modelled in our lives for others to follow.

Ways to keep bringing the excellence model to the fore in a worship team environment would be to ALWAYS pray together before ministering together and never depart from taking that time to gather, commit, forgive, praise and pull our hearts together. For teaching excellence also teaches that what we are involved with is Holy, not for a show or mere Christian entertainment, it doesn't even come close.

There was a day, not too long ago, when I ended up having about four hours of delays at an airport, which is not too unusual for many of us, but definitely NOT my favourite pastime. Anyway, as any good woman would do, I went to the airport shops to check out the buys. I finally found my way into this little costume jewellery store (guys, it's a nicer way of saying a 'fake' jewellery store). Anyway, I found the cutest little watch, with a thick white band and covered in fake little diamonds around the edge of the face, which was in the shape of a cross. Then I saw the price - $20. Must be a typo I thought, but no, checked with the assistant, and sure enough, $20 it was.

After thinking about it for two seconds, I decided the purchase was a good one and I walked out with the most blingy watch I'd ever seen... $20 well spent.

SO after about 2 weeks, it stopped working. What a rip off I thought, so I took the watch to the local watch repair man, and he took the cover from the back, and he then proceeded to have a little giggle. "I do hope you didn't pay much for this," he said. "There's nothing worth fixing in here."

Yes my little cute piece of time-keeping equipment proved to be useless. It looked good on the outside, really good, but there was nothing on the inside to keep it going.

Can you see where I'm going with this? Excellence coming from a secure place means simply your passion is connected to the truth and effectiveness of the outcomes. But careless actions, in any area of life that is applicable to you, will not bring about care-filled, God-honouring results.

Excellence for excellence sake is a trap, as then the comparisons start, and over time our convictions are watered down without us even realising. And soon we are just copying the copy of a copy that used to have our hearts all over it.

Daniel 6:1-3, 'Darius reorganized his kingdom. He appointed one hundred twenty governors to administer all the parts of his realm. Over them were three vice-regents, one of whom was Daniel. The governors reported to the vice-regents, who made sure that everything was in order for the king. But Daniel, brimming with spirit and intelligence, so completely outclassed the other vice-regents and gover-nors that the king decided to put him in charge of the whole kingdom.'

The goal we should be going for over everything else is an excellent spirit. And Daniel is our champion example in this regard. Daniel 6 says that eventually Daniel was put in charge of the whole kingdom because of his excellent spirit.

An excellent spirit will outrank any gifting, talent or charisma every time. It may take a little longer to get where you want to be going, but the results will be long lasting and bring strength for those coming through to lean into.

If you are going to achieve excellence in big things, you develop the habit in little matters. Excellence is not an exception, it is a prevailing attitude.[11]

Colin Powell

the great generational transition

VALUE EIGHT: HUMILITY

JAMES 3:13–16
WHO IS WISE AND UNDERSTANDING AMONG YOU?
LET HIM SHOW IT BY HIS GOOD LIFE, BY DEEDS
DONE IN THE HUMILITY THAT COMES FROM WISDOM.
BUT, IF YOU HARBOUR BITTER ENVY AND SELFISH
AMBITION IN YOUR HEARTS, DO NOT BOAST ABOUT
IT OR DENY THE TRUTH. SUCH 'WISDOM' DOES
NOT COME DOWN FROM HEAVEN BUT IS EARTHLY,
UNSPIRITUAL, OF THE DEVIL. FOR WHERE YOU HAVE
ENVY AND SELFISH AMBITION, THERE YOU FIND
DISORDER AND EVERY EVIL PRACTICE.

NIV

THERE ARE so many great traits that our churches and our teams should be known for:

Excellence

Unity

Hard Work

Being Joyful – Psalm 100: 'serve the Lord with GLADNESS'.

Being Prayerful people

Rich understanding of what it truly means to be a worshipper

Community - FAMILY

GREAT CULTURE OF POSSIBILITY

The list goes on and on.

But the one value we must never see as a low priority is humility.

GOD NEVER INTENDED OUR CHARACTER GROWTH TO BE of vague concern, but it is the most important and distinguishable feature of a true disciple of Christ.

The dictionary describes HUMILITY as the trait of being modest or respectful.

This is a very under informed description of this powerful word, for without humility, we actually have very little chance of sustained influence, as pride and humility, just like dark and light, have a hard time hanging out together.

Sounds heavy, but hey, Jesus was always great at confronting the hearts of mankind.

When humility is not present, the words - 'Your kingdom come, on earth, as it is in heaven' - become reversed to MY KINGDOM REIGN... my will, my ambition, my way or the highway!

You see, pride - which can appear so slyly, AND often in the form of self righteousness - has always been the downfall of the prominent, so called successful person.

What humility IS NOT:

It's NOT about putting yourself down;

It's NOT about letting people walk all over you and treat you like garbage. That's false humility, and has more to do with other issues such as lack of self-esteem and/or the outfall of disappointment;

Being humble IS NOT about allowing yourself to be minimised to FIT IN.

These ideas are all wrong, because YOU ARE OF SUCH VALUE TO GOD. These thoughts actually contradict scripture AND violate God's character.

In the C.S Lewis book, 'The Screwtape Letters' (1942), is a conversation between two demons, Screwtape, the very knowing older demon, teaching Wormwood, the young up and coming demon. It's an interesting take on enemy strategy (remember, it's fiction!). But they are discussing a strategy that would trap human beings into believing that a false type of humility seen to please man is all that is required as a Christian, their goal being to disarm even the finest people by seeing them crippled by self-doubt and insecurity, keeping their lives small and ineffective.

In times of transition this is the point where many people get stuck, either just for a moment, or tragically for some, this is the moment they never recover from due to being emotionally and spiritually hounded by doubt and unbelief. Can I tell you today, that this is not about you, these thoughts are from the pit of hell itself and you must realise it, and stand in the faith you KNOW is in you. A mustard seed worth of faith is a great start.

The stories of true humility are found in the 'WHO ME?' examples in the Word.

Take David for example... a kind-hearted shepherd boy, who even in his own Father's eye, didn't qualify or measure up to be included in the line-up of greats that were paraded before Samuel as possible candidates for King, and yet because God liked the appearance of David's heart - a humble, simple, devoted heart - God Himself raised David up, and caused what was obvious to the Lord, a pure heart, to be made obvious to man. When God called him forward, David had a 'WHO ME?' experience. Later in 2 Samuel, David prays an incredible prayer revealing the contents of his heart.

2 Samuel 7:18-21
'King David went in, took his place before God, and prayed: "Who am I, my Master God, and what is my family, that you have brought me to this place in life? But that's nothing compared to what's coming, for you've also spoken of my family far into the future, given me a glimpse into tomorrow, my Master God! What can I possibly say in the face of all this? You know me, Master God, just as I am. You've done all this not because of who I am but because of who You are—out of Your very heart!—but you've let me in on it." (The Message)

OK... take a breath. For a little pride check, here goes.

You can tell when pride is rising up in you...

When your question changes from, who me? to WHY YOU?? WHY NOT ME??

The time that David actually ended up getting himself into trouble was when SUCCESS and prominence brought about comfort and options, the two enemies of hunger, and pride began to breed in his very human heart.

Isaiah 66:2 says, 'this is the one I esteem, he who is humble and contrite in spirit and trembles at my Word'.

To be proud simply means to have an inflated view of yourself, so, you take credit for all of your accomplishments, believing that it could only have been YOUR efforts that could have paved your way, taking the mighty hand of the Lord out of the equation.

In Numbers 12, it says that Moses was a humble man, in fact, more humble than any other man on the face of the earth. I love that the Word even tells us that he really struggled with his confidence, stuttering as he spoke, never thinking he could stand in front of a nation to bring resolve and God's kindness. But there you have God's way. He honours the heart of man. In fact the Lord could trust Moses' heart SO much that it would not stray, that HE even allowed Moses to see Him and speak with Him face to face.

I WANT GOD TO TRUST ME TO SPEAK WITH HIM, over and over - clearly and simply - and then rather than it kill me, that I would be trusted with great mysteries and secrets of the Word of God... that they would be revealed to my heart.

DON'T YOU WANT THAT??

Even though the Word says He will lift me if I remain humble, that actually doesn't inspire me, but the ability to be trusted with His voice, now, that inspires me.

Humility means moving from self-centredness, to God-centredness.

Philippians 2 shares it with us like this:

Philippians 2:1-11
'If you've gotten anything at all out of following Christ, if His love has made any difference in your life, if being in a community of the Spirit means anything to you, if you have a heart, if you care - then do me a favour: Agree with each other, love each other, be deep-spirited friends. Don't push your way to the front; don't sweet-talk your way to the top. Put yourself aside, and help others get ahead. Don't be obsessed with getting your own advantage. Forget yourselves long enough to lend a helping hand.

Think of yourselves the way Christ Jesus thought of Himself. He had equal status with God but didn't think so much of Himself that He had to cling to the advantages of that status no matter what. Not at all. When the time came, He set aside the privileges of Deity and took on the status of a slave, became human! Having become human, He stayed human. It was an incredibly humbling process. He didn't claim special privileges. Instead, He lived a selfless, obedient life and then died a selfless, obedient death—and the worst kind of death at that—a crucifixion. Because of that obedience, God lifted Him high and honoured Him far beyond anyone or anything, ever, so that all created beings in heaven and on earth—even those long ago dead and buried—will bow in worship before this Jesus Christ, and call out in praise that He is the Master of all, to the glorious honour of God the Father.' (The Message)

C.S.Lewis said it like this, 'Pride gets not pleasure out of having something, only out of having more of it than the next man. We say that people are proud or rich, or clever, or good looking, but they are not. They are proud of being richer, or cleverer, or better looking than all the others. If everyone else became equally rich, or clever or good-looking, there would be nothing to be proud about. It is the comparison that makes you proud. The pleasure of being above the rest.'[12]

In 3 John, there was a guy named Diotrephes, who was SO intent on being prominent, that the Word says he LOVED to be first, greater than all, and he ends up devaluing and deliberately blocking the men of God in his community and the Word of God entrusted to them... Simply PRIDE, and a fierce determination to resist a change of heart.

But there is a sign that will reveal your true measure of humility, and that is

SERVANTHOOD.

Richard Foster writes, 'Nothing disciplines the inordinate desires of the flesh like service, and nothing transforms the desires of the flesh like service in hiddenness. The flesh whines against service, but screams at hidden service. It strains and pulls for honour and recognition. It will even devise subtle, religiously acceptable means to call attention to the service rendered. If we REFUSE to give in to this lust of the flesh, that is when we CRUCIFY it. Every time we crucify the flesh, we crucify our pride and arrogance.'[13]

Keep it simple friends... Servanthood

USE YOUR GIFT TO SERVE OTHERS.

Jesus was always focused on people and this is our example. To keep our hearts yielding to the ways of God and our mission to live In Him strong and sure… the GREAT COMMISSION is all about OTHERS.

Dying to selfishness is all about a death of the flesh. And all I can say about this is, whenever I feel like one aspect of this in my own life is nailed, wow, there comes another issue to deal with.

Philippians 2:3, 'Do nothing out of selfish ambition or vain conceit, but in humility consider others better than yourselves.'

1 Peter 5:5 instructs us to 'clothe ourselves with humility toward one another.' David was what in today's culture would be a super-celebrity, but in 1 Samuel 18, it says that 'all of Israel and Judah loved David, and he went out and came in with them'. In other words, he was approachable, not arrogant, but humble, serving others, doing life among the people.

HUMBLE YOURSELF before God

James 4:10 says 'to humble yourselves (feeling very insignificant) in the presence of the Lord and He will exalt you (He will lift you up and make your lives significant).' (AMP) The Word says 'He dwells with the humble and lowly in spirit.' Psalm 138:6 says that 'God actually distances Himself from the haughty.'

And when it comes to worship, it should be the most unselfish thing we do… for Him and through Him by grace. In other words, emptying ourselves of all we are, and offering our lives again, as a living sacrifice for HIS GLORY.

SO, how do we teach this? How do we infuse the value of humility through everything our lives represent?

We MODEL humility by our own behaviour, and practice humility through SERVICE.

You cannot preach this if you are not committed to living it. The next generation coming through has little time for inconsistencies between what we say and how we live. My own kids have taught me this as there have been times when, after I've taught something to the team, it has been tested in my own life almost immediately and aaahhhh, I failed the test! And that's what we love about family - no hiding there!!

Truth is premium lovely ones. This is not a show we are putting on called CHURCH. No, we are the hands and feet of Christ representing Him and all He stands for in our hurting world.

Humility is not thinking less of yourself, it's thinking of yourself less.[14]

Rick Warren

the great generational transition

VALUE NINE: GREATER THAN ADVERSITY

2 CORINTHIANS 10:3-6
THE WORLD IS UNPRINCIPLED. IT'S DOG-EAT-DOG
OUT THERE! THE WORLD DOESN'T FIGHT FAIR. BUT
WE DON'T LIVE OR FIGHT OUR BATTLES THAT WAY—
NEVER HAVE AND NEVER WILL. THE TOOLS OF OUR
TRADE AREN'T FOR MARKETING OR MANIPULATION,
BUT THEY ARE FOR DEMOLISHING THAT ENTIRE
MASSIVELY CORRUPT CULTURE. WE USE OUR
POWERFUL GOD-TOOLS FOR SMASHING WARPED
PHILOSOPHIES, TEARING DOWN BARRIERS ERECTED
AGAINST THE TRUTH OF GOD, FITTING EVERY LOOSE
THOUGHT AND EMOTION AND IMPULSE INTO THE
STRUCTURE OF LIFE SHAPED BY CHRIST. OUR TOOLS
ARE READY AT HAND FOR CLEARING THE GROUND
OF EVERY OBSTRUCTION AND BUILDING LIVES OF
OBEDIENCE INTO MATURITY.

THE MESSAGE

AGAIN, this may seem a strange value, but I have included it because when we know and understand which wars to fight, when we are made aware of the fact that the enemy of our soul uses contention and conflict within the Body of Christ so often to bring about discord, totally in opposition to what the Word of God teaches - then we become a stronger body, aware of enemy strategy.

Tension towards each other over trivial matters, and matters that are out of your control are useless in the end, and issues such as the greater disaster of people dying every day due to preventable disease is a war against humanity that we can do something about. OR, let's use our energies to come together to pray and seek God for evangelism strategies in our communities.

Our real enemy is a lack of knowledge of what is truly important, and a lack of understanding of how to work together. I have found myself in the middle of tension, getting really worked up over a matter, when in the end, I cannot even remember exactly what it was all about, and then I realise the enemy comes to kill, to steal and to destroy. What adversity brings in the end is complete distraction off the greater cause we are all working toward.

2 Corinthians 10 instructs us 'to use our passions correctly, to fight in the Spirit realm to pull down strongholds and arguments or any high thing that would try to exalt itself against the knowledge of God.'

Is unity possible? Can it really overcome adversity? Psalm 133 paints us a very real picture of what unity can achieve. King David knew from experience the disastrous effects of contention between individuals AND nations, he himself having to flee from Saul's hatred toward him. When, naturally speaking, you seem to have done all you can do to bring peace, and yet trouble still continues to brew, you have got to know how to PRAY. There are many moments in our lives that are totally out of our control, and these are the times we must remember to pray… to pray for those who lead us, to pray for those who we lead, to pray for wisdom in each situation, to pray for opportunity for reconciliation, to pray for great grace in troubled times, to pray for specific outcomes, and to persevere until we see a breakthrough.

I started to step up the TEACHING on this area of life to the team after our family found ourselves in a crisis moment that could only be described as terrifying, and we needed the hand of God to intervene.

When our youngest daughter Zoe was 5 years old, she was at home with us recovering from a tonsillectomy, having had years of consistent tonsil infections. It was a routine op, all went well at the time, she was weak, but getting stronger by the day. After a few days however, she started to go downhill, her colour changing to grey, her behaviour very strange, sleepy, unhappy. I kept taking her to the doctors but they could not see what the problem was.

Then at home in the middle of the night about 8 days later, Mark and I heard this strange noise. We ran to Zo, who was in bed haemorrhaging. We called the ambulance, we prayed, she was losing a lot of blood quickly and praise God, the ambulance was close by (the ambulance officer was SO incredible and ended up being a Christian). They raced to one hospital to stabilise her (met by another Christian doctor from our own church!), then they transferred her to a children's hospital for further treatment (where it seemed there were Christians everywhere!!). She responded well to treatments and we were home after a few days, EXTREMELY grateful to God and to all the people who have made medicine their life's work.

Our church was caring and gracious and looked after us all so well, she took a few weeks to get back on her feet, she was even visited by our church kids' mascot, 'Max'. To be on the other end of pastoral care was certainly humbling but oh so appreciated.

Interestingly, in the days and weeks that followed, I was SO surprised at the response of some of our young team, concerned and loving of course, but the questions that arose went like this: 'How did you pray?, What kind of words did you use when you prayed? Were you in a panic? Is it OK to panic in crisis? Does that mean we have no faith?'

And after a while I realised that this too was part of leadership, that they wanted to know more about real grass roots Christianity. Like I said in OPEN DOORS, the questions got intense; how to pray in times of strife, how to behave when life feels like it's falling apart, what is fake and what is not, what does an authentic Christian life look like if you haven't got 'it all together', can we still be the real deal?

And so, when I went back to our weekly rehearsals and teaching nights, I started to speak a little about spiritual warfare, what the Bible says about prayer, and how we can be on the front foot when it comes to seeing miracles in the every day moments in life AND in the times when you sense all hell is breaking loose over your world. We are growing continually in these areas of praying the Word over each situation, bringing intentional spiritual answers to our every need.

Leadership teaching is so fantastic, but it actually only becomes part of the fabric of who you are when it is tested, tried, walked-out and modelled. These life lessons are never ending, and never simple.

There have been times, of course, where we have prayed and believed for people to be healed and we never saw that healing take place here on earth. There have been times of dispute where people have disagreed and where we have tried to help bring resolution but to no avail. There have been times we've stood with some of these remarkable young people as they've had to stand by while their parents go through the hell of divorce, using their kids as a bargaining chip, their little hearts being broken. And so, you can see why we need to not just teach how to handle the easier things in life, but how to approach adversity and trouble in our world, still standing strong, speaking out loud the promise of the Word of God, announcing the Kingdom of God over every situation.

I have included this Psalm Study that we have previously done for our teams, which really helped cement the understanding of walking through trials and not being burned in the fire.

PSALM STUDY – CHAPTER 46

For the director of music. Of the sons of Korah. According to Alamoth. A song.

1. God is our refuge and strength, an ever present help in trouble.
2. Therefore, we will not fear, though the earth give way and the mountains fall into the heart of the sea,
3. though its waters roar and foam and the mountains quake with their surging.
4. There is a river whose streams make glad the city of God, the holy place where the Most High dwells.

5. God is within her, she will not fall; God will help her at daybreak.
6. Nations are in uproar, kingdoms fall; He lifts His voice, the earth melts.
7. The Lord Almighty is with us; the God of Jacob is our fortress.
8. Come and see what the Lord has done, the desolations He has brought on the earth.
9. He makes wars cease to the ends of the earth. He breaks the bow and shatters the spear; He burns the shields with fire.
10. Be still and know that I am God; I will be exalted among the nations, I will be exalted in the earth.
11. The Lord Almighty is with us; the God of Jacob is our fortress.
(Today's New International Version)

This Psalm is addressed to the chief musician, and I love that the Word of God puts value on the highly skilled in the areas of music and arts. In 1 Chronicles, we read that Zechariah, Eliab and Benaiah were to praise the Lord with Psalteries on Alamoth. As far as I can understand, this may mean to not worship through habit, or fall into the trap of singing in only one key, but to bring worship with intelligence in order to craft praises to appropriately express the fullness of the occasion. This explanation may not be completely accurate as the info available is scarce, but one thing I am confident of is that these ancient descriptions show that care, time and skill should be used when being part of any song to honour our King.

The first two words in this Psalm again bring so much confidence - GOD IS - our refuge, our strength, our VERY present help.

GOD IS... Do you actually believe beyond a shadow of a doubt that GOD IS all He says He is? I truly believe that if we grasped this revelation of who God is, our lives would look extremely different.

God alone is our All in All, our strength in weakness, and a very present help.

I was in worship at a funeral for one of the dear brothers in our church. Yes, it was sad, yes there was grief and heartache, but I had an overwhelming sense of GOD'S VERY present help. Very - more than your closest friend or relative, and even more present than the trouble itself. I think I've shared with you before that I'll never forget, just after my Dad died, that sense of sadness which was way too much to bear. My Dad and I were very close... I was his buddy, and even though life for him at the end was very confusing, he had Christ, and in that knowing, he had everything. Losing him was like losing my centre.

Weeks later I thought I would die of heartache. I was talking to God while I hung out clothes at the clothesline. Actually, I wasn't talking to God, I was CRYING out to God, when I literally felt His mighty arm, the arm of the Almighty rest around my shoulder to comfort me... VERY present, coming at just the right time. I did not want to move or breathe, or mess with that Holy moment. And I share this very private moment with you to encourage you today that He is our way through trial. Though many trials will try to come and defeat us, adversity at its evil best, we can stand strong knowing our God is near. Even when heaven and earth pass away, EVEN THEN, GOD IS!

Listen to this: 'Evil may ferment, wrath may boil, and pride may foam, but the brave heart of Holy confidence trembles not'. (Spurgeon of course!)15

We then find a Selah... pause, be calm, think for a moment.

The music set to this Psalm must have been quite colourful if you truly take in the words, I think after such a musical interpretation, the Psalmist needed a breath to bring calm, and to reflect a moment. This pause is not the fruit of dismay or doubt, but merely time to retune, set your instrument for deliberate music of victory in the midst of a storm, get ready for the music of the overcomers.

Now we are at the river, whose streams make glad the City of God. The City of God, Zion, whose streams are not intermittent, but ever flowing with grace and favour, rivers of life and joy, supplying all of our needs, bringing life and refreshing. The Church Is like the City of God. Its design, His glory, His purpose, His people, His message, His provision, streams of life running from it. Dedicated to His praise and glorified by His presence.

The City of God has always caused the enemy to rage, so it should be of no surprise that the Word says the heathen get angry about the streams of life. "How did this happen???" they continually ask. Their angry cries tend to swell in volume and intensity and beautifully, the Lord utters His voice, and the earth melts!!! GOD IS!!

Come and see is what the Psalmist declares. Come and see what God did to overthrow our enemies... our strength and shield, our ever present help. He was faithful yet again to His Word and His character. There is talk of all that the powerful voice of the Lord achieves... peace to war, end to strife, He crushes even the greatest of enemies until they cannot wreak havoc ever again. ONE word from God is all it takes to still the storm. That's why you need to have the Word of God IN YOU and realise that praying the Word is your great defence.

Then, the words we all know and so value... BE STILL AND KNOW THAT I AM GOD. The great I AM, says remember,

I AM.

He will be exalted among the heathen AND exalted on the earth.

Why then, do we hesitate to trust in our God... the great I AM?

If you truly trust, you've got to let go of trying to work everything out yourself.

Trust is something that people put confidence or reliance in.

Learn to let go, and trust God.

I found this song by the great reformer, Martin Luther. This is from a book written in 1866 entitled, 'Hymn Writers and Their Hymns' by S.W Christophers.[16]

'A sure Stronghold our God is He,
A timely shield and weapon;
Our help He'll be and set us free
From every ill can happen.

And were the world with devils filled,
All eager to devour us,
Our souls to fear shall little yield,
They cannot overpower us.'

Luther's explanation of Psalm 46 was, 'We sing this Psalm to the praise of God, because God is with us, and powerfully and miraculously preserves and defends His church and His Word, against all fanatical spirits, against the gates of hell, against the implacable hatred of the devil, and against all the assaults of the world, the flesh and sin.'

So I leave you with this thought… 'GOD IS'.

What IS GOD to you??

I pray He's your source, your life, your anchor, your breath, your reason, your song, your healer, your deliverer, your friend, your Lord, your overcomer, and your answer to adversity… PLUS the many other things I could list.

Be confident in His ability to hold your life in His hands.

For you arc His greatest pleasure.

The greatest glory in living lies not in never falling, but in rising every time we fall.[17]

Nelson Mandela

the great generational transition

VALUE TEN: FAILURE IS NOT FINAL

1 COR 13:8

LOVE NEVER FAILS...

NIV

IN OTHER WORDS

IF AT FIRST YOU DON'T SUCCEED, try, try again!!

I remember my mum saying this to me when I was a little girl (it's funny the things you remember as you get older!!)

But basically the core of this value is - never write people off! Don't discount people just because they made a mistake. This is NOT the way our God works and neither should we. Our God moves but He doesn't move on and leave us behind if we let Him down... no, He is committed to every one of us. Thank God I was never written off or condemned to life in the desert whenever I have made mistakes, and I'm sure every leader reading this can say the same thing.

It's called GRACE.

The sovereign message that silences condemnation and brings to the fore the reason for the Cross.

I have been a part of so many conversations where people have shared with me an experience of them trying to achieve a certain outcome, and then failing, and then losing personal confidence AND confidence from their peers. To be honest, it's a fairly natural reaction to get annoyed with yourself when falling short of a goal, OR, disappointing your employers, church leaders, your parents, those you hold in esteem when things don't work out quite the way you planned.

One of the great lessons I have learned is that when a mistake is made, a mistake made out of trying to do something worthwhile OR a mistake made out of a season of bad decisions, then we as leaders must learn to put the ball back in their hands quickly and with wisdom, and NOT discount the greatness in people or the strength of the GRACE of GOD. There has to be a WAY BACK plan for all who fall short of expectations (sounds like the message of Jesus to me).

The leaders of Disney, one of the most successful, creative, fun facilitators in the world have always said to their creative staff, 'failing is good, as long as it doesn't become a habit.' This is such a great environment for people to feel they can 'have a go', or try something new without being 'written off' if their idea doesn't work out.

Teaching people how to fail and recover is a must, as public blunders in small or large capacities have devastatingly taken SO many people off the path of their dreams for good!

In Deuteronomy 9 & 10, I was reading about the ten commandments, and about the two tablets of stone inscribed with the Holy covenant which it says were written by the finger of God Himself (can you even imagine!!) and my heart became totally captivated by the whole process of God finally having His intent for man to live by being preserved for all. Maybe it's just me but I would love to see God's handwriting!

Anyway, finally after forty days and forty nights these inscribed stones were handed over to Moses. Then something crazy happens, the people of Israel were acting corruptly and making carved images of empty gods for themselves to worship, and the Lord gets angry! He says to Moses He will destroy these people as they were SO rebellious and self serving.

Then Moses gets angry, and (can you believe this) actually threw the two tablets of stone to the ground and broke them!! Now, he finally prays and prays and gets God's attention (the Word says in Deuteronomy 9:19 that the Lord listened to Moses - how lovely is that?) and changes the course of history for these people. Talk about intercepting heaven and earth... BUT, I could not get over the fact that Moses actually threw that 'hand-engraved by God stone' that held God's requirements for us to live by, on the ground!

Do you ever remember breaking something of great value? Once we had a friend drop in for a coffee and just as he was leaving, he accidentally snagged the corner of a cloth I had on a side table on a folder he was carrying. This was no problem apart from the fact that an antique tea set that Mark had bought, when we got engaged, was sitting on the top... beautiful, hand made, delicate, one of a kind. You guessed it - the whole thing went flying and simply smashed into so many pieces. We all stood there looking at each other with our mouths open, and our friend started profusely apologising, and of course we said NO problem. But when he left, I had a little cry. But he felt SO bad!! I felt bad for him… oh that sinking feeling - mmmmm. I wonder how Moses felt? Ooooops! just dropped (or threw) the ten commandments.

Anyway, Chapter 10, the Lord fixes it all, the ultimate 'lets get back on track' plan, and says to Moses,

'Hew for yourself two tablets of stone like the first, and come up to me on the mountain and make yourself an ark of wood. And I will write on the tablets the words that were on the first tablets, WHICH YOU BROKE, and you shall put them in the ark.' (Deuteronomy 10:1-2 AMP)

So here we have the ultimate second chance moment for this time in history. Moses has already broken the first set of stones, now the Lord says, "here it is again, just like the first, BUT BUILD A BOX TO KEEP THEM SAFE IN!"

Ha! God is the ultimate Father at all times, and oh so practical!! But I love that Moses himself was not destroyed, just given a better way to do the same thing again. The heart of the Father is always to put us back on track, a little wiser, and just ever grateful for the second chance theory.

When you see people making continued unhealthy decisions, PLEASE LEADERS, have the courage to sit down and take the time and let them talk about what is going on. It is one thing when it comes to platform ministry and someone slips up, says something crazy, makes a musical blunder… talk about it in a healthy setting, get to it quickly and restore confidence. Otherwise a small imperfect moment can turn out to be a huge prickle in someone's soul. As is the way of life, small issues, when undealt with, turn into huge issues, and much harder to deal with.

When it comes to someone making very unhealthy choices that affect their soul, their behaviour, their family, their walk with God, again, you have got to have the strength and time to talk through the issues, and have a plan ready for them so that they can be restored. That's why I put the scripture at the top of this chapter - even when we fail -

LOVE never fails.

We are not here to judge, to condemn, to criticise, or even to know ALL the details… but we are here to love, encourage, lift, pray and be a support when resolve is weak. Jesus is called the ROCK - the rock of our salvation - meaning stability, ultimate strength and resolution. In being like Him, we too can be a sense of stability when the storms of life are brewing for those in our world.

King David, the great worshipper, even though he had murdered, committed adultery, as he humbled himself and sought purity of heart - God heard his cry… and the great warrior worshipper was revealed as just a guy who needed God. David still had to bear the fruit of that shocking season in his life, but the story of God redeeming man is actually what you remember about David's life. And the songs of worship that come from a life that has lived through a valley season… there are no songs like it.

1 Samuel 16:7, 'that the Lord sees not as man sees, for man looks on the outward appearance, but the Lord looks on the heart.' (AMP)

See, God is looking for repentance, which invokes true change.

The Father's love is SO incredible. My favourite story and picture of His costly love is found in the story of the Prodigal Son.

This son had disappointed his Dad, but the heart of this Father was always on the lookout, poised and ready for the son to return. Even before the son had come home, his mistakes were already swallowed up in the love of his Dad.

The Lord saw us… and came down. Just like this Father who, even as the boy was a long way off, saw him, and ran TO him, and fell on him and kissed his neck - the boy in the pig pen.

Many people wouldn't come close… they would only smell the stench of past mistakes, never getting close enough to get past the smell or the look of what was truly greeting them. A human being, FILLED with the promise of God.

But this Father's love is so, so strong… the son standing before his Dad with the stench of wrong decision all over him, and the Father clothes him with the finest, puts on a party, and welcomes him home.

'He looked beyond my faults and saw my need'.

I wrote these words in a song many years ago when I read Psalm 18 and got blown away again by God's commitment to us all, that He responds to our cries, and when we're in trouble, He is on the case.

Sometimes He moves heaven and earth to intervene, and other times he brings the answers through ordinary people like you and me. If we stand aloof to those people coming through in their faith, by judging their sometimes immature decisions, and icing them out when they make mistakes, then we shouldn't call ourselves leaders.

It's like parenting. The most wonderful and overwhelming privilege on the planet is to be entrusted to shape these lovely little lives. BUT, I can also tell you it is the most heart wrenching, emotionally exhausting, hard work there is.

We are not just leaders in the good times, no, you'll find the true leaders standing strong in the hard times.

Do you know that the Word of God says that they will know us by our love? John 13:35 says, 'By this all men will know that you are my disciples, if you love one another.'

LOVE is a BIG word. It demands so much of us even though it totally accepts us.

Another area under the topic of believing in people is, I think, you've got to be quick to realise which people issues are issues that are potentially very dangerous to the individual concerned, to your team, to the church etc... OR, if they are just simple mistakes that require a hug, a giggle, and an "it will all be fine mate" response.

I have had some absolute shocks to my system when it comes to people and 'secret' behaviours. But again, going to the Word, taking ALL our concerns to God in prayer, COVERING people as they go through times of having to make changes in their own lives and just believing in them on the road to recovery is critical. There have been times when walking through hard times with someone has taken weeks or months, other times it has taken years.

We have tapped into some amazing counselling programmes for those dealing with anything from marriage issues through to the outfall of sexual abuse, to dealing with the brokenness that results from SO many curve balls life can deal you. SO get good at not feeling like YOU need to know all the answers, but make use of the community and Christian-based services in your area. Again, this is what the body looks like, each of us taking our place for the benefit of others.

OK while we are talking about NEVER discounting people OR ourselves for that matter, a sense of humour is a must, and if you don't have one, this is an area you can and must work on.

The last few years we have worked closely with Dave and Joyce Meyer, leading the worship for some of their events and missions endeavours and it is a huge, huge, honour. They are one great couple, and what you see presented is TRULY who they are.

Anyway, we were in Nashville, leading the worship, and we were having one of those amazing meetings where you seriously feel like heaven is in the room and you sense such a liberty with the worship, a real freedom and joy. The team travelling with me from our church have all travelled with me over many years and we have a certain flow and trust when we are leading people in worship that we definitely lean into when playing. So, at such a critical moment during one of the songs, I called for a key change (a musical lift) and half the band saw me signal this, and half didn't. The music was loud and confident and heading for such a powerful crescendo and - *#!*#! - you guessed it, we hit with cyclonic strength a crescendo of musical mess, played with such confidence and volume that even the stars in the sky made a slight adjustment!

After we recovered we nervously laughed, waved goodbye to the Holy Spirit (joking!!) and kept playing. Later on I commented and said, 'well, maybe people just didn't notice??' The band just looked at me and said, 'Darls, we are in Nashville!!' (music capital of the world), and sadly, with MySpace videos, it was no time before many others saw the moment. (At least these moments have a great way of keeping our pride in check!!)

But, as bad as it was, in the scheme of things, it was nothing but a really bad memory! A long time ago, I don't think I would have let it slip through my soul so easily. I would have beaten myself up for not leading the band well and letting down the people who had invited us. But thank God for a little bit of maturity, time and a sense of humour. Now I can even write about it, laugh again, and just smile at God's sense of humour that he would even use my life at all!!

Once I was speaking at the Billy Graham Training facility in Ashville, USA, and right at a pivotal, passionate moment, my shoe got caught in the hem of my jeans and I literally fell flat on my face! The band were sitting there not knowing whether to laugh or cry, when one of the guitarists turns to the production manager and says, and I quote, 'Should we go help her?' 'NO', he answered, 'she doesn't like fuss. But I will just go quickly and make sure I got it on video!!'

We laughed so hard that night (and so did everyone else who was at The Cove Training Facility). I am actually getting embarrassed again just typing this onto my computer!!

These kinds of mistakes hurt our pride rather than our future, and as leaders of others, just always be growing in your maturity to know quickly what kind of mistake you are dealing with, and treat it appropriately.

There have been times when, as a leader, I have made incorrect and soft decisions about getting people up on the platform to minister when maybe their life choices were not God-honouring, and other times when I have been too hard on people, making the entry point for service just too high. But as long as you are able to say sorry and admit mistakes, as long as you have a heart to gather and not condemn, as long as you truly do know that as a Christian, what God is looking for is all about the heart and not about the gift, as long as you are all about inclusion and not exclusion, then all will be alright. I just thank God for the Holy Spirit, leading and guiding, teaching and speaking. Where would any of us be without friendship with God?

1 Peter 4:8 'Above all, love each other deeply, because love covers over a multitude of sins.'

History has demonstrated that the most notable winners usually encountered heartbreaking obstacles before they triumphed. They won because they refused to become discouraged by their defeats.[18]

B.C. Forbes

the great generational transition

VALUE ELEVEN: THROW OUT THE OLD?

2 SAMUEL 23:3-4
GOD'S SPIRIT SPOKE THROUGH ME, HIS WORDS
TOOK SHAPE ON MY TONGUE. THE GOD OF ISRAEL
SPOKE TO ME, ISRAEL'S ROCK-MOUNTAIN SAID,
"WHOEVER GOVERNS FAIRLY AND WELL, WHO
RULES IN THE FEAR OF GOD, IS LIKE FIRST LIGHT
AT DAYBREAK WITHOUT A CLOUD IN THE SKY, LIKE
GREEN GRASS CARPETING EARTH, GLISTENING
UNDER FRESH RAIN."

THE MESSAGE

'OUT WITH THE OLD, IN WITH THE NEW' I heard myself say as I was joking around with some of the other guys who had been part of our team for a long time. We all nervously laughed, but I was left with a nagging sense that this needed to be dealt with in me, not used as a new catch cry to hide behind whenever I felt insecure. Mmmmmmm, Lord help me. Lord forgive me.

This is a HUGE subject, for again, history proves that many who approach a change of season in leadership, and really need to bring through 'next genners', often are not secure enough in who they are WITHOUT holding onto the same position, and so they end up jumping ship TOO early and ridiculing the process in some kind of self-defence.

The scripture at the start of this value is literally the last words of King David, as he readies himself for the ultimate handover, and speaks on the IMPORTANCE of God-fearing leadership... saying that the fruit of this kind of leadership is like the rains after a hot day, refreshing, and life giving.

It is easy to simply hold onto a position or title for dear life, holding on WAY too tight, or you may even acknowledge that change is imminent, but you will leave in a flurry of drama, never to be available to help or coach, and many times, totally ambushing your own next powerful season.

For those of you who are feeling the need to bring change, my advice to you is to make sure that you are LEADING the process WITH STRENGTH out of security and DON'T jump ship. Be a gracious captain, at least until you know that the ship is stable!! Yes, it will look different to how you have always known, and sound different to what you have always heard, but no less heartfelt and God-honouring.

It's amazing, if you can be strong and generous and motivated by the greatness coming up around you, that it creates a grand state of stability within the team, and that in itself is inspiring. Now we all have moments of sensing a use-by date over us, but seriously, you need to get in the Word of God, and be bigger than these simply dangerous thoughts.

Proverbs 1:33 says, 'But whoever listens to Me will live in safety, and will be at ease, without fear of harm'.

The enemy seriously takes delight in destroying the territory of the soul, and negative thoughts about oneself left UNCHALLENGED and undealt with, will be enough over time to simply take you out of your own race.

I have a friend who is so disciplined in her home and in her wardrobe, when it comes to 'out with the old', that whenever she purchases something new, she ALWAYS gives or throws away whatever it is she was replacing. Fantastic way to keep your home organised, but SO does NOT translate when we are talking about people and seeing them flourish in life. But to treat people like commodities at all is an incredibly damaging way to live and not God-honouring in the slightest.

If people only ever hear from you when you want something from them, then it is not a mystery why you would find gathering the troops hard.

The strength and beauty of the church has always been her passion, her sense of safety, her ability to shine even in the darkest of places… but also, her diversity, her ability to embrace every single person. She is SO unique! Every nation, tribe and tongue - that combination of wisdom and enthusiasm, experience and naivety - the older speaking life and lessons to the younger, and the younger bringing energy and enthusiasm, pioneering in a new way.

When the time comes for a shift to happen, in whatever way shape or form that may be, there does NOT have to be bloodshed and an abrupt ending to a season for it to happen at all. But usually, due to a lack of truthful communication, complications tend to take hold leaving unanswered questions and hearts disappointed - usually it is simply perception setting the tone rather than fact, but that is the result of relationship without communication.

So lets talk about COMMUNICATION… what's NOT to say??

Try sustaining a marriage without communication, doesn't work for long. Try raising your children without communication, you end up leaving all their value forming years up to whoever the loudest voice is in their world, sometimes this even ends up being the television. Try growing an alive and sustaining relationship with God without communication and prayer… you'll end up feeling like heaven is very silent.

Smooth transitions are always dependant on thoughtful process, and thoughtful language.

If you read Deuteronomy 33, it's the story of Moses' last days, and when he realises that this will be the last time he gets to speak over the people he has led for so long, he speaks absolute blessing from his heart over the children of Israel and from verse 6, he starts naming each of the tribes, and spends his last moments on earth pouring himself into the future, speaking the Word of God and the heart of a father over every one of them. He did not hold anything back, but loved God and people right to the end.

Leadership is about example, vision, hope,

AND LEGACY,

and not just talking the talk, but walking the walk. Moses was so very loved, and after he died in the land of Moab, the people wept for Moses for thirty days.

Remember when I said I had talked to the team about their dreams and goals for their lives? It was after that time that I was truly motivated to start lifting my own speech, to raise the bar higher, as what used to be impossible when I first started was now quite possible and I hadn't made the inner adjustment and neither had many of our team. I think this is why sometimes you NEED to almost shake out the old, because if they won't recognise or embrace the now it is very hard for change to come.

But as one Christian leader said to me... 'Good on you Darls... Better you making the changes than having them done to you!!'. Amen to that!!

And so we, very much 'on purpose' as leaders, started lifting our own language and speaking with more energy to solutions rather just than the problems, and speaking about leading nations rather than just our own communities. We started speaking about seeing miracles, not just dreaming about them as a 'one day' concept, we started disciplining ourselves to live with renewed vigour and passion with whatever it was that was in our hands.

I have got to say that it didn't take long for the atmosphere over not just our team but each of us individually to start to lift, and it was SO infectious!!

We still live in the fruit of this decision today… but the fun part is that those coming into this environment notice it, embrace it (as it is stimulating), and adopt it as their own way forward.

I have heard great testimonies since that time, of people like myself, who made a decision to challenge what had become the acceptable way, and start dreaming again of what could be.

One of the great advantages of this mindset, is that it definitely gives you inner strength to launch into some brave and unchartered waters. But that is what the Word of God is full of, great stories of ordinary men and women who knew their own inadequacies but believed for something greater – actually believing in that still small voice you hear at times saying YOU CAN DO IT even when all evidence may say otherwise.

And so the legacy of the undone begins in your bloodline…

My own grandparents are devoted, passionate Christians, who in their late nineties are still dreaming, still living independently, still driving (aaahhhhh!!) and still encouraging all their kids and grandkids and great grandkids in the ways of God.

They stand on the doors in their home church each weekend and help look after the 'old people', they still send us all gifts at Christmas and take the time to call wherever we may be to check up on us and make sure we are doing great.

It was when my nan was in her eighties that she had an encounter with the Holy Spirit that changed her forever, even though both her and pop have been Christians since a very young age.

They have continued to inspire all of us kids to the core on so many levels, especially when it comes to

KNOWING and SERVING GOD,

and what it really means to

LOVE YOUR FAMILY.

Every time we are with them, they take the time to speak blessing over our lives, to pour themselves out, as if it would be the last time we'll see them or speak with them. It is their commitment to smooth transition that I admire. The last time my pop saw my second daughter Chloe, who is very passionate about architecture, he hugged her and hugged her and said that he probably wouldn't be around for the opening of her first building, but she was to know on the day her first building opens, that he is so very proud of her. What a kind man... no regret, not withholding love when it will help define a young person's dreams, no speaking negatively over the future and the world our children are growing up in.

No, just the Word of God and His promise over all that is in our hearts. My nan played the organ in church for so many years - faithful, loving God, but when the time came, she was SO gracious... 'time for the young ones', she said.

Now that's generosity at its purist.

The old loving the young, and being the bridge for their dreams.

I know that one thing that really encourages some of the younger guys in our team is that I am still here, still leading worship, still writing and dreaming and creating, but just standing to the side and cheering others on as they take their leadership place, whether in our own home church environment or beyond. I have had to swallow my pride and tackle my own thought processes on the journey, but the end result is so worth it.

One of the wonderful things that people don't tell you about is the amount of trust and friendship that develops over time and over the journey of life that you end up taking with people. Actually, I believe many people miss out on this incredible gift because they don't stick around long enough, or leave their post at the first sign of conflict. Conflict is inevitable if you are doing life with PEOPLE!! God did not create us to be robots, but human beings with thoughts and feelings and connection with God Himself.

So conversation is

PREMIUM

if you want to do life with others. But so is dying to self, as often, our opinion is not what is needed, but a spirit that prefers others.

Matthew 5:9 says, 'Blessed are the peacemakers, for they will be called the sons of God'.

I do understand that there are many healthy reasons people move on, but there are also many unhealthy reasons, and it is to this I refer.

To be honest, this is one of the reasons that I have personally found SO much joy in seeing others fly, because once you know them and love them for more than what they do, but for their hearts and dreams and potential and simply who they are, well, the sense of fulfilment in release is very deep, and again, one of the great surprises along the road of leadership.

To walk with people through hard times and good times, times of great blessing and times of great loss, just like your natural family, this family of God is developed and strengthened through imperfect seasons and seasons of great momentum. And in this understanding of time-tested leadership, I have discovered the very real and intensely deep joy of relationship.

There have been times along my own journey of late, when some of us who've been around a while have been less needed as far as the platform goes...
oh my gosh, I have begged people, challenged people, and tried in my own strength to ensure a sense of worth in people even though we are making room for change and growth. But you do come to understand that sometimes people do transition well, and sometimes they don't.

In the end, it is their own decision, their own choice - you as a leader can only do so much. And everything under heaven has a time and season, to recognise the season you are in is probably one of the great skills to possess as you get older.

I honestly think it is much easier short term to simply walk away and become one of the 'misunderstood ones', rather than becoming one of the pillars of strength for the journey, the wise siblings who count it all joy to share life knowledge, the ones who are committed to the race to the end, even as the role of WHAT you do changes. I honestly THANK GOD it does change!!

I have loved my own journey (mostly) to date, but am excited that the new looks like walking on water. I am so grateful for that!

I have discovered this whole new chapter, this whole new purpose to my last 20 or so years, as I see the reason that the worshipping heart is so critical becoming very clear in my inner man. And I know that this next season of worship AND justice, the message of true worshippers taking their place in seeing broken humanity restored, is so alive in me that it is like the whole last season of life was simply preparation for the new, and it feels STRONG and GOOD.

In my heart of hearts, I also have prayed over years that the Lord Himself would give me a revelation about what it means to serve the next generation, not just to be a leader or someone they can look up to, but actually serving their dreams, and their visions, and their new ways of doing things.

Challenging? Initially, yes.

Inspiring? Absolutely yes!

When I see people around me, half my age, carving and pioneering their God-given pursuits, my heart is full and I am continually challenged to keep dreaming and creating, not allowing my own processes to become stale and nostalgic.

But I am still me, you are still you.

Don't apologise for your season, embrace it,

bring the very best of YOU to the table.

So let me ask you a question?

How are you doing with the whole deal of making room for others, and for many of us, actually handing over much of what used to be, to walk into all that is in front of us?

One thing that may help - I realised very quickly that while my hands were filled with the old, God could not fill them with the new.

Doing what we've always done brings a level of comfort that can be hard to let go of, not to mention that feeling out of our depth is emotionally risky, stepping again into unchartered waters means we cannot lean into tried and true methods (thank you Jesus!).

So, I am not saying it will be easy, but I guarantee it will not be as difficult as you think. If your heart and mind are not filled with vision (go back to Value Three), then this also makes it really hard for you to let go.

Life affords no greater responsibility, no greater privilege, than the raising of the next generation.[19]

C Everett Koop

the great generational transition

VALUE TWELVE: PEOPLE

PSALM 103:6-18

GOD MAKES EVERYTHING COME OUT RIGHT; HE PUTS VICTIMS BACK ON THEIR FEET. HE SHOWED MOSES HOW HE WENT ABOUT HIS WORK, OPENED UP HIS PLANS TO ALL ISRAEL. GOD IS SHEER MERCY AND GRACE; NOT EASILY ANGERED, HE'S RICH IN LOVE. HE DOESN'T ENDLESSLY NAG AND SCOLD, NOR HOLD GRUDGES FOREVER. HE DOESN'T TREAT US AS OUR SINS DESERVE, NOR PAY US BACK IN FULL FOR OUR WRONGS. AS HIGH AS HEAVEN IS OVER THE EARTH, SO STRONG IS HIS LOVE TO THOSE WHO FEAR HIM. AND AS FAR AS SUNRISE IS FROM SUNSET, HE HAS SEPARATED US FROM OUR SINS. AS PARENTS FEEL FOR THEIR CHILDREN, GOD FEELS FOR THOSE WHO FEAR HIM. HE KNOWS US INSIDE AND OUT, KEEPS IN MIND THAT WE'RE MADE OF MUD. MEN AND WOMEN DON'T LIVE VERY LONG; LIKE WILDFLOWERS THEY SPRING UP AND BLOSSOM, BUT A STORM SNUFFS THEM OUT JUST AS QUICKLY, LEAVING NOTHING TO SHOW THEY WERE HERE. GOD'S LOVE, THOUGH, IS EVER AND ALWAYS, ETERNALLY PRESENT TO ALL WHO FEAR HIM, MAKING EVERYTHING RIGHT FOR THEM AND THEIR CHILDREN AS THEY FOLLOW HIS COVENANT WAYS AND REMEMBER TO DO WHATEVER HE SAID.

THE MESSAGE

ONE OF THE GREAT quotes from my grandfather goes like this:

'As I look back over my life, and all the twists and turns, the unexpected - the good and the bad - I can now see the hand of God in it all.'

Talk about perspective. (Yes, these are the same grandparents who, when Mark and I celebrated our 20 year wedding anniversary, sent us a card that read, 'don't worry, the first 20 are the worst!') More perspective.

It almost seems too obvious to write the word 'people' under the heading of 'value', but I felt quite compelled to do so, as I wanted to spend some time speaking about YOUR worth, not just the worth of those coming behind you and those around you. Essentially this book was created to give each leader at least a few extra tools to assist in the transition period, helping people to rise and take their place. But without you actually sensing a strong future forward for YOU, then it can be quite displacing. Transition often is.

Jeremiah 29:11 says, 'For I know the plans I have toward you declares the Lord, plans to prosper you and not harm you, plans to give you a hope and a future.' This scripture was not just given to everyone else, but to you.

In Philippians 3:13 we are encouraged to focus all our energies on what is lying ahead, not getting stuck or emotionally tortured by what is in the past.

We've got to stay focused.

But let me ask, are you confident that you have a successful future?

After having many conversations with leaders in transition, it seems that letting go of what is in the past is very hard when you're not sure about what is ahead. The mystery is often too much for people, and so hang on to the past they must.

Perhaps this is you. But my dear friends, letting go and walking confidently forward is called faith. And your language of faith is so important for YOU at this time. Caring for your soul, dreaming, writing down your thoughts, in fact all the tools that we are talking about to use to encourage others, you need to apply to yourself, and have faith that God Himself has established you IN Himself, by His power and grace.

Romans 16:25 from the NIV says, 'Now to Him who is able to establish you by my gospel and the proclamation of Jesus Christ, according to the revelation of the mystery hidden for long ages past, but now revealed and made known by the prophetic writings by the command of the eternal God, so that all nations might believe and know Him.' Seriously, here is the Lord, guaranteeing His Word over your life by His Name, and His Covenant. Assurance is yours today, God is on your side and making a way.

But a way to where? And this is where many get caught out, start drifting, and forget that yes, God is all about people, but not just others, he is also for ME.

For myself, I sat down with Isaiah 61, and I read that prophecy over my own life, out loud. I spoke it over my influence and my time, over the unspoken imaginings within my heart, and asked God to speak with me, to walk with me, to teach me what this scripture looked like in my own day-to-day.

And then I took out a new notebook, clean with potential, and prayed, and wrote. The fact that I was in transition wasn't a mystery, but walking it out well AND walking with purpose into where God was calling me was a mystery yet to be revealed. And the more I spoke with different people in my world about my questions, the more opinions I was receiving and as well-meaning as they were, it was not God's voice coming at me but just popular, and often very strong, opinion. I realised that to shepherd other people well through transition and beyond, I had to hear from God myself, to listen, and to really hear, and to follow. God is all about people… remember this.

So Isaiah 61, 'The Spirit of the Lord is upon me' chapter, is all about people. It's about how the Lord will use Jesus through you and me to bring freedom to people held bound… and to announce freedom to prisoners, and comfort all who mourn, and the list goes on. The Spirit of the Lord has anointed you and me for this task, for this season. We are enabled, equipped, smeared with His ability, anointed for the task at hand. We are anointed to preach the good news. He has sent us to the broken, to bring light to the dark, to comfort, to provide for the grief-stricken, to bestow crowns of beauty over those who feel ugly, to bring gladness and praise that unashamedly displays the Lord's splendour. It says we will rebuild ancient ruins, and restore ruined cities, and that finally righteousness and praise will spring up before all nations.

So, hear my heart, if what is before you looks bleak or simply unclear, read this chapter of scripture and ask God to fill the chambers of your heart with renewed vigour for His purpose. The first day that I did this, I ended up with pages and pages of thoughts and then I started to meditate on them, really praying that the Lord would lead me to define the things that would delight His heart more than anything.

So, let me get very vulnerable and give you a peak into my own list and writings.

Some of what ended up on my list looked like this...

The Spirit of the Lord is upon me because:

- I have a complete conviction about my marriage, and what this means to me and my family and the generations to come. This conviction crafts my choices, I will not compromise, Mark and I are in this God-journey together and our marriage will ebb and flow only to the tune of the 'BECAUSE factor' in our lives.

- I have a complete conviction about raising our daughters... and again, this will shape my decisions, keep me from compromising, and help me to live a life that is worthy of them following. I will lead them to the Lord and His will for their lives.

- I have a complete conviction about the local church and the worship of God... that truth and creativity would resound from the earth in praise to God... that I will serve in the house of God all the days of my life. I will not be distracted by good things, but be captured by His presence, that His presence will define my life, not great opportunities or the praises of man.

- I have a complete conviction about bringing solution to the many innocent people around the earth who are literally starving, downtrodden and poor, the many or-phans and widows who are caught in wars, the aftermath of war, natural disaster, and situations beyond their control. Fill my hands with answers Lord, and fill my life with influence to bring change… that I would be found trustworthy!!

• I have a complete conviction about raising and releasing the next generation - that my role within the framework of leadership is my life would be committed to seeing others fly! A new day for the body of Christ.

OK, I will leave it there. The rest of my list is more personal, but perhaps this will help you start to set your sights on things ahead, and help you to stay sharp and focused. And now, whenever I feel a little shaky, I confidently go back to my 'BECAUSE FACTOR' list, and reset my sails, speaking the WORD OF LIFE OVER THE ATMOSPHERE IN MY OWN HEART.

And when you start to feel weary, remind yourself that you are anointed for the task at hand. Start to worship and pray, fuel your love for Jesus, because if your heart is not full, your hands will get tired.

Selah…

The gospel is all about people, God loving us, His children…

His children finding Him and loving Him…. and His children loving each other.

Our lives should be a Hallelujah from head to toe.[20]

Augustine

the great generational transition

VALUE THIRTEEN: GENIUS

PHILIPPIANS 3:12
NOT THAT I HAVE ALREADY OBTAINED ALL THIS, OR
HAVE ALREADY BEEN MADE PERFECT, BUT I PRESS
ON TO TAKE HOLD OF THAT FOR WHICH CHRIST
JESUS TOOK HOLD OF ME.

NIV

I WONDER what it was like for King David to die with such a grand vision in his heart to construct a great house of God, knowing he was not to be the one to build it, but his son Solomon was. I wonder how Moses felt, handing such a climax of his journey over to Joshua, with God actually saying to Moses that He would show him the future, but it was not his to occupy (Deuteronomy 34:3-4).

I wonder how you feel about literally letting go of much of what you have believed God for, and actually handing it over to someone else?? AND, I wonder how you'd feel handing something over, only for the 'next genners' to take it to a whole new level and make it SO much greater?

What if those coming through are actually made of GENIUS!

Let me tell you, the chances of genius in your midst are very high. I have sat in rehearsals and listened to some of the new songs being written by some of these younger men and women, and sometimes I seriously go home in shock at the brilliance! I read scripts being written, look at artworks being created, fashions being constructed... and I am inspired!

Don't be nervous, look around, genius is everywhere, just waiting for its appointed time.

Romans 1:20, 'For since the creation of the world God's invisible qualities—His eternal power and divine nature—have been clearly seen, being understood from what has been made, so that men are without excuse.'

You know, we've got to get good at inspiring the greatly talented in our midst, and if you have trouble doing that, go back in your mind to the times when you sensed God leading you to the place where you are today, to the times where God's gentle but very persuasive voice echoed deep in the chambers of your heart... and you'll find a continued thread joining it all together. You will remember when God and man spoke life into you, breathing hope into your thoughts, the push behind your soul that keeps doubt at a safe enough distance away. For whenever God speaks, He is calling us onto a path that always results in restoration, salvation, creativity and people's hearts and lives being reconciled with the Father. He never leads us to a path of self destruction or purely self-fuelling or self-promoting exercises.

We are all a part of the eternal story being written, and whenever I sense a feeling like walls closing in on what part I have to play in this, I will go back to some of those heaven moments where my life course was truly affected, and where the heart of God resonated with mine, putting my feet on solid ground and showing my heart the truth of God's word. It doesn't take long for the insecurities to start melting away in the light of His glory. I can see where the historical heroes got it right, knowing that rather than their part in the divine jigsaw puzzle of life being minimised, that they all were living in moments where there was a sense of history being written and their moment being a significant chapter in the greater story.

And this is what we have to remember!!

Hebrews 12:1 says it all. 'Therefore we also, since we are surrounded by so great a cloud of witnesses, let us lay aside every weight, and the sin which so easily ensnares us, and let us run with endurance the race that is set before us, looking unto Jesus, the author and finisher of our faith, who for the joy that was set before Him endured the cross, despising the shame, and has sat down at the right hand of the Father.'

I love that story about WALT DISNEY, who planned and dreamed Disneyland and didn't even live to see it become what it is – yet, I kind of think that he did see it. He saw it in his mind, in his heart and in every fingerprint of who he was. He talked about it, drew plans consistently, made plans for its eventuality… but his very positive legacy of the undone meant that what was in his heart was completed and taken to the next level by others.

You see it with King David and Solomon. David had it in his heart to build a house as a place of rest for the ark of the covenant of the Lord. But God said to him that he was not to build it, that He had chosen David's son Solomon to complete the work. Here's the greatest thing about this, and it is two-fold. Firstly, David encourages Solomon just SO much, saying 'Be strong and courageous and do the work, do NOT be afraid or discouraged, for the Lord your God, My God, is with you'. I LOVE that, and he gives Solomon all the how to's, but along with this, and most importantly, David's leadership continues with giving him the greatest advice of all.

Check out 1 Chronicles 28:9. It says, 'And you my son Solomon, acknowledge the

God of your father, and serve Him with wholehearted devotion and with a willing mind, for the Lord searches every heart and understands every desire and every thought. If you seek Him, He will be found by you, but if you forsake Him, He will reject you forever. Consider now, for the Lord your God has chosen you to build a house as the sanctuary. Be strong and do the work.'

So the law for the agenda of the heart was established as the Lord requires, and David's stunning prayer in 1 Chronicles 29 brings the story to a climax of thanksgiving.

I clearly recall the day our nation heard the news that we had the privilege of hosting the Olympic Games in the city of Sydney. We were all so excited, and the plans for stadiums and huge sporting venues started to be aired throughout the media outlets as the excitement gathered momentum. I sensed straight away that these stadiums would eventually be used for the glory of our God, and that there would even be a day when they would be too small. Isn't it amazing, that for us to take a worship event into a stadium is still such a buzz and you stand there wondering how on earth this happened, and what this does for the heart of the church at large is so encouraging as you realise that the Spirit of the Lord is moving in such a powerful way, and that His church is alive and well.

But you know, for our children, this is SO normal. They talk about filling all the gigantic football stadiums, not just the stadiums of 30 and 40 thousand. No, what is crazy great for us is just their beginning, and you see Ephesians 3:20 come into play - 'more than you could ever hope or dream for... such is the nature of our God'.

I see man-made genius everywhere around me. I see it as a true reflection of the creative nature of our God. I see it in architecture, I hear it in music, I feel it when I am moved to the core during a scene in a movie, I taste it when I am eating something exquisite, and I touch it whenever I feel incredible fabrics and surfaces.

And when I see genius in the house of God, people using their gifts to express devotion, I can hardly stand it because it is so good!!

I have seen many genius types drift in and out of church as they have sat there wondering how on earth they could contribute… whether they would be judged if they are a little different purely because they approach art and its outworkings with more intensity than others.

With genius in our midst, we've got to learn to get out of the way, to listen to the intensity of thought that is usually expressed passionately and with definitive intent, AND, you've got to let the process of how the outcome is achieved be different than in the past.

It's hard to do, let me tell you, especially if you can see a smarter way to achieve the outcome, BUT, you've got to learn that there are many ways to a great creative outcome. I have learned that different is often just that, DIFFERENT. Not worse or greater, just different.

LEADERS… GET GOOD AT LOVING THE DIFFERENT.

So, if you are leading others and sensing brilliance amongst you, are you encouraging it and not trying to control it? And if you are one of the ones that are coming through (woohoo!), are you keeping your agenda clean so that God can trust you with all that is in your heart AND all that is still being developed??

Pretty amazing hey?

And because our God is a really good dad, he will not give to us anything that is too much for us to handle.

But here's the thing about genius and when it comes to the greatly gifted… WHAT they bring is often so easy for them. They make it look easy, they often can not explain how they do it because it IS A GIFT! Their gift has often made a way, and we all can get blinded (in a great way!) by the gift. But for all the leaders, this is probably where you'll find your own challenge and that is in the discipling of genius.

This has been one of my personal, toughest, leadership lessons to date, the pastoring of genius, walking people through success and through creative disappointments. I've heard many leaders say that all their problems would be answered in church if they had some more 'well known, crazily talented people' in their team. But I wonder if you are secure enough, AND confident enough, to pastor and challenge the areas of their lives that would need to be challenged.

I've heard the story retold and retold about sports genius, musical genius, any kind of genius you can think of, and Pastors retelling the story that to get these genius types to come and be part of a church community is very hard. The problem though is not just about the genius thinking he can play by a different set of principles. No, the problem is also perpetuated from leadership down… leaders being intimidated, leaders being a little infatuated, leaders USING the giftedness to bolster their own position among their peers, etc.

I know I am making a blanket statement, but to be honest, I have seen this happen so many times, that the exception is truly the exception.

And so we end up with genius being all around us, but we need leaders who are grounded and large-hearted enough to simply accept the brilliance and let it shine, AND, who will encourage strong disciplines such as making the Word of God a priority in their lives, building strong church and family life and making it priority, and guiding them through success if it comes, and sticking with them if it doesn't. Until then, I doubt that you will be trusted with this privilege often. But wouldn't it be wonderful if you could. That anyone in your community who was gifted in any area knew that they could come to you KNOWING you could be trusted to bring the finest Godly counsel to their lives, with self-interest not entering the equation, but God's purpose at the core.

Leadership… We are all part of this amazing race, running in our own lane, but running with a baton to pass on beautifully to the next runner. In my relay, I want the baton that I hand to my next runner in this life relay to be a hot, on fire baton… a baton that represents miracles, a baton that represents a journey that was carved out in faith, filled with creative expression and filled with continued hope and expectation. I DO NOT want to hand over a baton that is tired and worn out, disillusioned, and resentful.

C'mon leaders, stand tall, speak with grace and courage, release others, and trust God with your own life.

When genius comes into your midst, it is crazy to think there is not room for all of us.

When serving the Lord, what we are all involved with is a HOLY calling, not a life of whimsy or spiritual goosebumps, but a walk of great value, and it is to be treasured. Your life is a life that matters - every season matters - and without you, without me, contributing our piece of the journey, and us living with an understanding that it cost Jesus everything for us to be free, then the rich and real values of this voyage called LIFE would be minimised to simply chance and fate.

In Revelation 15 this song was sung, and I pray you hear it sung as a great testimony to all that God has done, is doing, and is going to do:

'Great and marvellous are Your deeds, Lord God Almighty. Just and true are Your ways, King of the ages. Who will not fear You O Lord and bring Glory to Your name? For You alone are Holy. All nations will come and worship before You, for Your righteous acts have been revealed.'

There's a genius in all of us.[21]

Albert Einstein

the great generational transition

VALUE FOURTEEN: HEARTS OF FLESH

MICAH 6:8
'HE HAS SHOWN ALL YOU PEOPLE WHAT IS GOOD
AND WHAT DOES THE LORD REQUIRE OF YOU? TO
ACT JUSTLY, TO LOVE MERCY, TO WALK HUMBLY
WITH YOUR GOD.'

TODAY'S NEW INTERNATIONAL VERSION

THE GREAT LOVE OF GOD FUELS OUR BEING

THE GREAT COMMISSION FUELS OUR DOING

Ezekiel 11:19, 'I will give them an undivided heart, and put a new Spirit within them, I will remove from them their heart of stone, and give them a heart of flesh'.

Do you remember the day you gave your life over to serve Christ, and opened your heart to salvation, and your heart became new, an eternal spiritual transformation, from stone to flesh?

It is interesting though, in the midst of an information overload, sometimes frenetic environment, we can so easily become an event-driven, over-busy, experience-driven generation, and our hearts of flesh slowly become unfazed almost by the cry of humanity… and the heart changed by the love of God seems to find its way to its own Christian bubble… and the heart of stone stands just around the corner, waiting to fill its former space.

What a tragedy of the heart, and yet we have the absolute antidote to hardness of heart, which is simply found in serving others, and loving Jesus.

Meeting need head on, living to lift the lives of others, going on this journey will intentionally arrest a complacent or inactive emotional space, and over time, bring the core of the heart back to life in all its fullness. The hard thing here is that a heart fully alive is a painful organ to live with! A heart alive in Christ sees need and has to do something about it; a heart alive in Christ is soft toward the voice of the Holy Spirit and is more likely to respond with an obedient yes; a heart fully ALIVE is a dangerous centre to work from.

A heart fully alive recognises seasonal shifts and prepares well for the changes, in fact readies itself and others who may be affected, with open communication and a continued commitment to fuelling those they can with life. Again I say, what an honour, and what a huge responsibility. But when a heart is hardened simply by having to do life with all its challenges and hurdles to overcome, the heart has this incredible ability to get stoic, a self-preservation mechanism maybe that protects itself as much as it can from being hurt.

The result of that toughened heart is that it can become cynical, untrusting, it is able to see dire need and feel nothing. It can live in continual violence and still be seemingly unaffected. I thank God that when He does a work in us it is an inside-out transformation, not an outside-in demonstration. That the heart, as much as we get almost tired of hearing how important its health is both in the natural and in the spiritual, if our core, our engine room is faulty, then it is only a matter of time before other associated factors in our lives start to be affected by this.

I have seen kids who have lost their entire family due to genocide in Rwanda, end up having to get up and get going and fend for themselves on the streets until either someone comes to help, or death comes and brings relief. And because this is the expected LOT in their lives, their little, beautiful hearts become so tough so they can cope with what tomorrow brings, IF tomorrow comes.

The heart is such a resilient muscle.

Micah 6:8 is a great revealer of the heart of God when it firstly asks the question,

'so what REALLY is it that the Lord desires from you?

More sacrifices?

More public display of your devotion?'

The answer that is given is STRONG and straight to the point, and pulls to the surface without any hesitation the core and heart of the Bible.

'To do justly, and to love mercy, and to walk humbly with Your God'.

And this is why when it gets down to the call and purposes of God for each of our lives that the state of our HEART is critical to the whole story. For without His power at work in our hearts always, we easily become unaware of the need all around us, or within us, and we go through the motions of mindless Christianity, or become a slave to a works-based theology, which may never even be spoken, but maybe in you is real.

This comes to the fore because we get over-concerned about pleasing others, the chronic syndrome of being driven because of your need to get approval from those around you, rather than being compelled by the convictions you have to serve Christ. This is a lesson that every one of us has to learn along the journey some-where.

One of the traits that I personally have loved about the generations coming through is that often they are not happy to invest their time into something without being assured that it is worth the time and effort needed to see the task accomplished. And I love what we've seen in churches around the globe - that there is an inten-sity and increased passion to see missions endeavours that result in people being helped, spreading like wildfire, often being led by young, radical Christians who have made it their life goal to live out Micah 6:8.

One of our dear friends is a young man named Hugh Evans, the founder of a great charity called the Oaktree Foundation.

Oaktree Foundation is an aid and development organisation run entirely by young volunteers, who are committed to empowering developing communities through education in a way that is sustainable.

Do you know that Hugh's whole goal was to make sure he had handed over the leadership of Oaktree by the time he was 26. AND he did. Remarkable!! And every volunteer is under the age of 26 as well. We have attended some of their functions, and the passion and ability to outwork their goals is remarkable.

But this is the cry of young people everywhere - that they want to be involved in something greater than themselves, that they want to be involved in something that helps relieve human suffering, local and global.

Paul O'Rourke, the CEO of Compassion Australia writes in the book 'Blessings of the Poor':

'The poor who know Jesus are wonderful ambassadors for what is valuable in God's Kingdom. They trust in Jesus because they must; their very existence depends on His provision. They are unencumbered by the world's deceptive trappings of pride, envy, and self sufficiency. They work hard, are thankful for what they have, and focus on the things that are important: faith, family and friends.

The poor have taught me many things including humility, dignity, the sacrifice of worship, faith, hope, joy, generosity and contentment. I have discovered that you can't out-give either God or the poor.'22

What Paul reminds us, is that in our outworking of God's heart through bringing relief and answers in the developing world, we also have much to learn from those suffering, as the truth of life is quickly revealed in living in abject poverty.

It is essential that we are part of raising children and teams that are not only aware of what is going on in the world, but that at the core of our language is resolve, which will take all of our lives and beyond.

There are many ways to lead this, and I am sure many of you reading will have great missions programs you can highlight through your teams, send teams over-seas to work in the field hooking up with well trusted ministries, sponsor children through connect groups or friendship circles, and always PRAY for those who are suffering and persecuted.

When it comes to truthful worship, it always requires a choice - will I or won't I? And as we get real and vulnerable before the presence of the Almighty, then He brings about change IN us. I do know that when God grabs your heart, it doesn't have butterflies attached to it, it is actually very uncomfortable. It is always choice, and because of an encounter with Christ, it will always bring about change.

For years I wrestled with the uneasy question in my spirit - what is the change for?

And I finally came up with the simple Holy Spirit answer. It is for people. All of our worship belongs to God; all glory belongs to God, and He uses our lives that slow-ly mirror Him, to take His love in varied forms to the planet. And when it comes to anyone on the platform, this MUST be taught.

I believe with many artists, world famous 'musos' and singers, actors, etc, the reason they don't cope in life is that our human bodies were never designed for glory, we were never designed to receive it, only to give it to the one who breathed life into us. When you receive it, and keep on receiving it, it will eventually destroy your soul.

But God's passion, well put it this way, He's certainly not sitting in heaven going yes, more glory for me, more glory for me.

His passion is you.

His passion is me.

His passion is our neighbours, our families, the kids sleeping on the streets, the prostitutes who are trying to make a living to feed their drug habit that simply silences the raging pain within.

This is our God.

I have used the illustration about washing people's feet so often. We come and lead people in worship and metaphorically, we come washing their feet, taking their troubled souls and simply pointing them to Christ through the restful fragrance of truthful worship.

Jesus, when He sat at the well with the broken woman in John 4:24 - I love that He was far more interested in the life and healing of a broken woman than His own reputation, and hers. And her own story continues to blossom through this God encounter - and Jesus starts to describe to her a living water that was available to her, that would sustain her through all of her life, and everything changes.

The economy of heaven is people, that's all we can take with us - OTHERS.

The Word says,

'Thy Kingdom come, thy will be done on earth as it is in heaven',

so the value is people, but the atmosphere is worship. Revelation 14 gives a little preview into what the sound of heaven is like... extreme worship for sure!

My creative juices get going as I see and hear this scene, like a Spielberg special effects showcase.

Verse 2 says, 'And I heard a sound from heaven, like the roar of rushing waters and like a peal of thunder and the sound I heard was like that, of harpists playing their harps. They sang a new song before the throne and before the four living creatures and the elders, and no one could learn the song except the 144,000 who had been redeemed from the earth'.

I LOVE IT... the sound of praise like the rushing of mighty waters. Revelation 5 says 'to Him who sits on the throne and to the Lamb praise and honour and glory and power forever and ever'... the sound of heaven. So we get the sound of heaven, and we get to practice here on earth,

BUT what is the sound of the earth?

It's a groaning, a weeping, the hollow sound of life with no hope, the sound of the broken. It's the sound that actually implored the heart of God to send Jesus.

There's a big gap my friend, a great divide that almost looks impossible. But there is our role right there - to bridge the gap, generation to generation, the redeemed to the unredeemed. A bridge taking people from darkness to light.

This is the reason our lives matter... to tear down the walls of injustice and see the dawn break over our earth. And this is what our teams need to know and not be afraid of, but be inspired to be the change.

This is why I get SO passionate about our worship NOT being clothed in performance, but being raw and real, for God does not need perfection of gift, but authenticity of heart. This is the place in your heart where you'll find

COMPASSION

springs from. Compassion, the emotional stop sign that Jesus most often responded to.

The story of the good Samaritan is another one of my favourites, and the part I love the most, is that the good Samaritan LIFTED the life of another, he secured him, he paid for him, he took care of him. He saw the need, responded with kindness and followed through. I notice that the Samaritan must have also had margin in his day TO help, rather than just not having time, and rushing past.

To be known as a Christian leader on any level and not to be known for the love in our hearts is an absolute tragedy, but one that can be remedied. We don't want to just be singers of songs, but lovers of God who use the whole of our lives, our Romans 12 understanding of worship, to say,

"Hey, this injustice stops with us".

Our heart and mission to relieve human suffering means for the rest of our lives we will live with our hearts fuelled in worship to have our lives poured out in service. I pray for continued wisdom and revelation, and for great grace and kindness, as justice makes a way for those who until now have only known grave suffering.

YOU HAVE SHOWN US
Words and Music by CompassionArt

VERSE 1:
You have shown us O God
What is good
You have shown us O Lord
What You require
You have heard all our songs
How we long to worship
You've taught us
The offering You desire

CHORUS:
To do justly
(and) To love mercy
(and) To walk humbly with You God

VERSE 2:
You have shown us
The riches of Your love
You have shown us
Your heart for those in need
You have opened our ears
To the cries of the poor
You have called us
To be Your hands and feet

BRIDGE:
To the oppressed and the broken
To the widow and the orphan
Let the river of Your justice
Flow through us

How wonderful it is that nobody need wait a single minute before starting to improve the world.[23]

Anne Frank

the great generational transition

FINALE: A STUDY OF DEVOTION

DEVOTION… Committed love, dedication, enthusiasm, religious fervor, act of devoting.

- Devotion is such a beautiful word, it rolls off the tongue and actually sounds like it means. But devotion is not just a word that pleases the senses, devotion is a word that demands something of us. Something that requires more than our mind and our body, but all of our heart and soul.

Devotion is born out of revelation, out of a divine transaction that has gone on deep within, requiring the one who has had the experience to dig deeper, to give more of themselves, to apply the energy and priority that is often traded for more menial moments to be given in earnest affection.

And it's the word DEVOTION that I am going to apply to our journey of worship, as to me this word describes closely the heart voyage that is part of understanding the wholehearted commitment of loving, serving and following Christ.

Worship cannot be contained to music, or fully played or described by the psalmist, although these are all part of our desire to express love in song to God.

Over 40 Psalms alone ask us to SING unto our God, for He can never be praised enough. But let me talk you through a brief biblical overview of worship - its intent, its origin, and its purpose.

The exhausting thought for me always is that although God Himself is complete without us, He still chooses to be incomplete without us. His love is so crazy, so endless, so all encompassing that our love toward Him delights Him, even though He has the universe at His feet. That He knows our names, the hairs on our heads, the content of our hearts, our gifts, our talents, the colour of our eyes, our failings, our hopes… yes, this is a God who cares for His kids, and who inhabits our praises with the fullness of Himself.

Worship is born out of revelation, and response to God's initiative.

John 4:19, 'We love Him because HE FIRST LOVED US.'

Before we knew Him, He loved us. Before we called Him Lord, He called us. There is nothing, no height, no depth, that can compare to the great love of God.

And with that in mind, we worship. And not just in DEED, but in SONG.

To sing the song of the redeemed, the song of our hearts, to join this manifesto of song that spans from the beginning of time to now. The song of the sons and daughters of God, trying to express something of the magnitude and wonder of the saving grace of God.

The worship of God is timeless and eternal, right from when Adam and Eve and their family at the end of Genesis 4 leaned in closer to God in thanksgiving for remembering them, through to the morning stars joining in on the choruses in Job 38. King David displays his CARE about worship in 1 Chronicles when he puts together the huge choir and orchestra for tabernacle worship, Mary is singing the 'Magnificat' in Luke 1, and Jesus sings a hymn of praise with the disciples in Matthew 26.

The song of God has continued throughout history - man pouring out of the deep places in his heart, reaching out to a God who sent his precious son Jesus Christ, who through the resurrection power of the cross displayed a love so great that separation from God was given solution, and the veil that had separated us was torn from top to bottom, making a way for us on every level.

1 Peter 1:6-9
'I know how great this makes you feel, even though you have to put up with every kind of aggravation in the meantime. Pure gold put in the fire comes out of it proved pure; genuine faith put through this suffering comes out proved genuine. When Jesus wraps this all up, it's your faith, not your gold, that God will have on display as evidence of his victory. You never saw him, yet you love him. You still don't see him, yet you trust him—with laughter and singing. Because you kept on believing, you'll get what you're looking forward to: total salvation.' (The Message)

Truthful worship, through persecution and beyond, refined as pure gold, and the song goes on.

What we are part of today has been building for generations. It's the song of faith, not our giftings or abilities, but the sound of the Spirit of God alive within us that makes the song, the stance, the mystery alive! And as He is pursued and welcomed among us, the felt evidence of the Holy Spirit among us continues to build momentum, calling the lost home and stoking the fires of hearts that have become lukewarm.

The significance of His glory and His presence is of eternal and immeasurable weight.

From age to age, everlasting to everlasting.

• 'Worship is our responding to the overtures of love from the heart of the Father. Its central reality is found 'in Spirit and in Truth' It is kindled within us only when then the Spirit of God touches our human Spirit. Forms and rituals do not produce worship, nor does the formal disuse of forms and rituals. We can use all the right techniques and methods, we can have the best possible liturgy (a form and arrangement of public worship laid down by a church or religion), but we have not worshipped the Lord until Spirit touches Spirit… singing, praying, praising, all may LEAD to worship, but worship is more than any of them. Our spirit must be ignited by divine fire'.[24]

Richard Foster

True worship is revealed when we declare God's worth - *'weorthscipe'* which in essence means 'ascribed worth'. Worthship! It is not an expression of devotion that can be contained to the mind, even though this frustrates many believers who would feel safe if this was the case. It is an expression released through the heart, in as much as our language of thanksgiving and adoration are given voice, via this gateway of love.

Psalm 18 paints a vivid picture on the heart of God Himself being moved by the plight and ache of humanity, and how His LOVE for us fuels His motivation over everything. Without some sort of understanding of God's love for us, it is difficult to let a genuine THANK YOU flow.

So, rather than trying, trying, trying to love Him more, the key is to simply meditate on His great love for you. It will not take long at all before you sense a new understanding of what 'entering His gates with thanksgiving' actually means.

It seems that we struggle with such a love that accepts us as we are, that loves us beyond our faults, and loves us to life.

In the performance culture of our world, you can actually tie yourself up in knots trying to be 'good enough' to worship. And most people say, 'I just don't deserve this great love to be poured out over my life.' And it's true, we don't deserve it. It is God's longing to be with us.

John 1:14 says that 'the Word became flesh and dwelt among us.' We did not earn it or deserve it, but we are loved and have been made right with God through the blood of Jesus. God sees us and knows us, and yet still desires to be with us.

When I was first saved, I was in my own little world, and was very, very disheartened. I didn't expect God, I didn't behave and try to do good things and hope some higher power would accept me... NO, God found me, and I found Him, and my little world was changed forever. I still find it hard to fathom the power that lives in me, and why God chose me. But He did. He chose all of us, and filled us with His presence and the same power that raised Christ from the dead. Go figure.

This is ultimately when grace stands there and protects us from ourselves, the TRYING too hard generation. The generation who in being so desperate to get it right, actually end up a very long way from where the simplicity of truth begs us to journey. None of us could ever be good enough, clever enough, right enough, or whole enough, and that's the point. We NEED a Saviour, and through His saving grace, our response in worship is a surprise, but the closest thing to heaven we'll experience here on earth.

Worship is a supernatural action, the response of humanity, the created to the Creator.

Isaiah 43:18 says that we were all created for His glory - not for ours, for His.

Worship is a faith response, a response to distinct revelation. It carries many strands of devotion, from the most simple to the most sublime.

The active life of a worshipper pours itself out in a sacrificial manner, starting in obedience, and finding itself in adoration and consecration.

The worshipper finds themselves in a position of servant, heart and hands ready to do the will of the Father.

Worship, at every level, always means God, and the priority of God the Father, the precious Holy Spirit, and Jesus Christ. And because of the nature of God, He turns it around and makes it about us, His Spirit at work in and through us.

Through worship, humanity enters into that great life of the spiritual universe which consists in the ceaseless proclamation of the Glory of God. Creation has always been poised, ready to delight the heart of God.

In worship, we are kept in constant remembrance of the unchanging, ever Holy nature of God, and every single life submitted to this influence is changed.

Some of the Biblical truths about the worship of God are:

• That we all worship (actually this is one fact that universally, anthropologists agree about).

• That the gospel is a call to worship, laying down our lives and taking up His cross.

• Philippians 3:3 says 'we worship in the spirit of God and boast in Jesus Christ'.

• Worship involves the whole of our life, Romans 12

- Worship, when offered from the body, both gathered and scattered, is a continual reminder of our shared story and identity in Christ.

- Worship is the promised future of earth and heaven. Rev 5:13, 'then I heard every creature in heaven and on earth and under the sea and on the sea and all that is in them singing, to Him who sits on the throne and to the Lamb be praise and honour and glory and power, for ever and ever.'

- Worship is so valuable, that there is a constant battle on for our worship.

Satan, in Matthew 4, tries to entice Jesus by his cunning words, his empty words when he says 'kneel down and worship me'. Of course Jesus has the ultimate victory, but when you are vulnerable, be on the lookout for the enemy to come to see your passions exchanged. In Isaiah 14 he says, 'I will ascend higher than God and all His stars', the age old story of pride.

- Worship identifies which Kingdom you belong to.

In the end, it all comes back to love. His love FIRST for us, and our response of LOVE back to Him. It's easy to sing about love, to share it, to talk about it, but to receive it freely is one heck of a mind blower!!!

I believe there are no prayers like prayers offered in worship.

1 Thessalonians 5:17, 'BE UNCEASING IN PRAYER (praying perseveringly) THANK GOD IN EVERYTHING (NO MATTER WHAT THE CIRCUMSTANCES MAY BE, BE THANKFUL AND GIVE THANKS) FOR THIS IS THE WILL OF GOD FOR YOU who are in Christ Jesus.' (AMP)

In Revelation 5, it describes this scene in heaven, elders holding a harp (depicting worship) and each of them also had golden bowls full of incense, which are the prayers of God's people. I love this scene as prayer and worship comes before God, and songs are sung throughout heaven declaring His majesty and reign, and that He has won the victory over every need.

Some people pray loud and confident, bold - they don't even give thought to who may hear. Others prayers are offered in whispers and moments of total silence.

Many prayers are offered wrapped in music and melodies that allow the prayer to be fully engaged where otherwise they may find it harder to enter the courts of God. Never underestimate the power of your prayers, and in being committed to raising up a powerful team of prayer warriors, where the Word is prayed and sung with clarity and conviction.

I pray that a revelation of God's love is the utmost in our hearts and lives, and with that revelation comes an increased burning desire to see others receive this love. And that is where worship starts to kick into a whole other level, as the worshippers become truly LOVED, and confidence in Christ and His power at work in us shapes our lives, our language, our behaviour, our songs, our time and our passions.

Unfortunately, all of us can be found making our conviction of what it means to serve and worship Christ, our own personal latest theology and can so easily discount or judge others who are outworking His life in them in different ways.

Method, skill, atmosphere, tried and true technique - this will never take the place of God-encounter, never can and never will.

The truth is that the Word is full of challenge and encouragement to trust in the Lord with our whole heart and the rest - the sound, our style, our musical preferences, etc - can and must morph and change as every generation brings a new song and a new fabric to the rich tapestry woven for generations in this Kingdom realm.

Yale professor Nicholas Walterstorff once said that, 'each people group, each generation, needs to be able to express its sense of worship in its own voice, in a way that resonates deep in the soul. As our culture keeps changing, these are not issues that the church can pretend will go away. Just because a sound is not our style, doesn't mean it's not sacred.'

As we near the end of this book, I want to just remind each of you of the power of doing everything we do motivated by His great love at work in us.

Mother Teresa said, 'it's not what you do but how much love you put into it that counts'.

As we lead and encourage all those who are coming through, remember that it is in loving that we are most like Christ, because

GOD IS LOVE.

It's not just worship, music, giving, justice, songs, hymns or choruses etc, it is all about LOVE.

The Word says this, 'The whole law can be summed up in this one command, love others as you love yourself.'

John 3, 'For God So LOVED... that He gave'.

LIVING LOVED is a powerful God-breathed concept, that if we would get it... wow, that's revolutionary!!!

Love means legacy - without love, it's just existence: Worship without love is just music; relationships without love are simply acquaintances; a congregation without love is just a club; a church worship team without love is just a band, a song without love is just a jingle. LOVE is the ingredient. A problem tackled without love ends in war; a pursuit of Christ without love ends in religion; a gaining of wealth or inheritance without love ends in greed.

LOVE is the ingredient.

Please know today how much each of you are loved. Even if you don't feel it, you cannot change the fact that you are. Let's live loved, lead loved and serve loved, and with strength and grace, pass on all that we know to the next generation.

Let me finish with a story...

Many years ago, on my first trip to Rwanda, I walked back into our hotel after a long day out in the field. My heart was breaking, filled with an ache of frustration, not knowing how to do more, but knowing I must. The word must have got out that we were staying at this hotel, as the room was filled with orphans who were now young adults, who were obviously Christians who loved to worship, but had lived really tough lives. Children raising children…

The words echoed in the foyer… 'Mumma, Mumma', and these kids came at me from all sides, touching, hugging, crying, 'Mumma, you came'. Somehow, the music of our church had come to them years before, bringing comfort and strength, and a sense of security. Later in conversations they shared how, when they were looking for a mum, I sang to them, and had sung them to sleep ever since, teaching the Word of God, and speaking life over them.

I was humbled and challenged that day, and a sense of resolve was placed deep within my Spirit as I realised that every choice we make has a chance to influence the next generation one way or the other - either up close, or from afar.

If I was standing in front of you now, I would sign off by saying how much I truly love and believe in each of you, and even more so, how God Himself loves and believes in each of you. Let's do whatever it takes to handle this season we have been entrusted with, with grace and strength, and pass on all that we know to the next generation. Humanity is counting on it.

With all my heart,

Darlene Zschech.

Ephesians 3:20-21, 'God can do anything, you know—far more than you could ever imagine or guess or request in your wildest dreams! He does it not by pushing us around but by working within us, his Spirit deeply and gently within us. Glory to God in the church! Glory to God in the Messiah, in Jesus! Glory down all the generations! Glory through all millennia! Oh, yes!' (The Message)

notes

1. Robb Report, Worth Magazine – Feb 2004

2. Marianne Williamson - "A Return to Love" 1992

3. "Our God Reigns" written by Delirious? – Curious? Music UK 2005

4. John O'Donohue – "Eternal Echoes: Exploring our Yearning to Belong"
   2000 Cliff Street Books

5. Henry David Thoreau "A Weekend on the Concord and Merrimack Rivers"
   Dover 1849

6. "God Of This City" by Chris Tomlin / Passion Worship Band 2008

7. Norman Vincent Peale "The Power of Positive Thinking" 1982. Ballentine Books

8. Peter Marshall – "The Prayers of Peter Marshall" by P & C Marshall.
   McGraw Hill 1955

9. Eugene H Peterson – "A Long Obedience in the Same Direction"
   Intervarsity Press 2000

10. John Wesley – statement commonly known as "John Wesley's Rule"

11. Colin Powell – "The Powell Principles: 24 Lessons from Colin Powell,
    A Legendary Leader" written by Oren Harari. McGraw Hill Professional
    Education Series 2003

12. C S Lewis - "Mere Christianity" Macmillan 1952

13. Richard Foster – "Celebration of Discipline". Hodder & Stoughton 1999

14. Rick Warren – "The Purpose Driven Lfe". Zondervan 2002

15. Charles H Spurgeon – "The Treasury of David" Pilgrim Publishing 1870-1885

16. Martin Luther – "Hymn Writers and Their Hymns" by S W Christophers. Anson Randolf NYC 1867

17. Nelson Mandela – "Long Walk to Freedom" Macdonald Purnell 1994

18. B C Forbes – "Forbes" by Bertie Charles Forbes. Forbes Inc 1980

19. Charles Everett Koop

20. Augustine – "Historical Memorials of Canterbury" by Arthur P Stanley. London John Murray 1883

21. Albert Einstein

22. "Blessings of the Poor". Various authors. Compiled by Paul O'Rourke. Strand Publishing 2007

23. Anne Frank - "Diary of a Young Girl". Doubleday & Company 1952 (USA)

24. Richard Foster – "The Celebration of Discipline". Hodder & Stoughton 1999

the great generational transition

THANK YOU ...

To my husband Mark, serving God together forever, what a ride babe!
I love you completely. Thank you for your loyal Godly leadership in our marriage
and home. You make 'following' a joy and an adventure and I am up for whatever
the rest of our days look like! xx

To my beautiful, generous-hearted children and family.. thank you for cheering me
on in every endeavour... I am blessed to be yours and love you so... xx

To our dear dear Hillsong Church family and friends, Pastors and mentors.
For many years I have stood in awe of every single part of our church, the past,
the present and the future. Thank you for the joy of being able to do life in
church family.

To the crew at 4B Media and The HOPE Office, Margie, Jared, Gracie and
Rachel... Kathy, Josh and the team at The Grove Studios... wow! The journey
is incredible! Thanks for your willing hearts and your passion to bring answer to
human suffering. By God's grace this is just the beginning.

To the ever patient Camille and Miffy... what do you say to the women who edit
you, pray for you, cover you and make you sound better than you are? Girls, I am
forever grateful... thank you.

To all our lovely friends... every day I thank God for you... you make my heart
smile... thanks for your patience xx

And thank you to Pastor Brian Houston, Pastor Tommy Barnett, Joyce Meyer,
Pastor Bill Hybels, John Maxwell, Pastor Jack Hayford, Graham Kendrick and the
many leaders who inspire and input into our lives...
Mark and I are eternally grateful.

And thank you Lord for saving me, restoring me, and filling my life with a new song
to forever declare Your worth. All Glory and All Honour, All Power and All Praise to
You forever and ever...

Australian Darlene Zschech is acclaimed all over the world as a singer, songwriter, worship leader and speaker, most notably for her involvement in the music from Hillsong Church, Sydney over many years. Although she has achieved numerous gold albums and her songs are sung in many nations of the world, her success simply stands as a testimony to her life's passion to serve God and people with all her heart.

As a songwriter, Darlene is perhaps most famous for the chorus "Shout to the Lord", a song that is sung by an estimated 25 to 30 million churchgoers every week and has been covered by at least twenty other artists. "Shout to the Lord" was nominated as Album of the Year for the 1997 Dove Awards and was nominated as Song of the Year for the 1998 Dove Awards. In 2000 Darlene received a Dove Award nomination for Songwriter of the Year and received the International Award for influence in praise and worship.

In addition to "Shout to the Lord", Darlene has written over eighty songs that have been published by Hillsong Music Australia alone. In 2005 Darlene released another album "Change Your World", which features a new arrangement of Michael W. Smith's worship song "Agnus Dei". Involved in the CompassionArt project 2008, she was so honoured to be allowed the privilege of writing with some of the most generous-hearted worship writers and leaders of our day. Darlene is also passionate about raising and training other worship teams and writers, and has written three books which include 'Extravagant Worship', 'The Kiss of Heaven', and her new book, 'The Great Generational Transition'.

Many years ago Mark and Darlene made a life commitment to do whatever they could to bring answers and relief to human suffering, and one of their great joys in life is to work with Compassion International, serving the world's poorest of the poor children.

It was a Compassion trip to Central Africa in 2004 that prompted Mark and Darlene to initiate Hope: Rwanda, a global endeavor designed to bring hope to a nation seemingly forgotten since the horrific genocide of 1994. The 100 Days of Hope (April 6 – July 15, 2006) project was strategically coordinated to cover the same 100 days that saw approximately 1 million people viciously slaughtered. Hope Rwanda (www.hoperwanda.org) continues to bring hope and healing to Rwanda, and a new 'HOPE' has spread into Cambodia. The HOPE team are excited about all the future endeavours that continue to gather great momentum.

Darlene and Mark live in beautiful Sydney with their three daughters, Chloe and Zoe, Amy and son-in-law Andrew. While they travel extensively and have the honour of working and ministering alongside amazing friends around the globe, family remains Darlene's supreme delight. As she says, "First and foremost I am a woman who simply and wholeheartedly loves Christ, and serves Him through loving my family, serving the church, and speaking up for those who cannot speak for themselves."

HOPE:Rwanda

HOPE is a faith-based, non-profit organisation that brings together church, government, NGO's, private enterprise, heathcare and individuals, to provide practical solutions to countries devastated by war, genocide and poverty.

Our primary objective is to assist developing nations reduce poverty, achieve sustainable development, and to bring spiritual strength and social justice to every segment of society.

HOPE aims to empower people for reconciliation and complete restoration of hope and dignity.

How are we bringing Hope?
- Village of Hope: purpose-built village caring for widows and orphans in Rwanda.
- Hope Medical: cardiac surgery, hospital construction and health education
- Education: nursery & primary teacher training, resourcing and school buildings.
- Poverty reduction: micro-enterprise development, leadership training, business mentoring, business leaders' workshops
- Support: indigenous churches and humanitarian groups already working in Rwanda.

www.hoperwanda.org